ATOPOLOGICAL TRILOGY

ATOPOLOGICAL TRILOGY
DELEUZE AND GUATTARI

Zafer Aracagök

dead letter office

BABEL Working Group

punctum books ∗ brooklyn, ny

ATOPOLOGICAL TRILOGY: DELEUZE AND GUATTARI
© Zafer Aracagök, 2015.

http://creativecommons.org/licenses/by-nc-nd/3.0/

This work is Open Access, which means that you are free to copy, distribute, display, and perform the work as long as you clearly attribute the work to the authors, that you do not use this work for commercial gain in any form whatsoever, and that you in no way alter, transform, or build upon the work outside of its normal use in academic scholarship without express permission of the author and the publisher of this volume. For any reuse or distribution, you must make clear to others the license terms of this work.

First published in 2015 by
dead letter office, BABEL Working Group
an imprint of punctum books
Brooklyn, New York
http://punctumbooks.com

The BABEL Working Group is a collective and desiring-assemblage of scholar-gypsies with no leaders or followers, no top and no bottom, and only a middle. BABEL roams and stalks the ruins of the post-historical university as a multiplicity, a pack, looking for other roaming packs with which to cohabit and build temporary shelters for intellectual vagabonds. We also take in strays.

ISBN-13: 978-0692403723
ISBN-10: 0692403728

Cover Image: Rhida Dhib, *Entré chien et loup* (2013).

Table of Contents

Foreword: The Undecidable :: i

by Manola Antonioli

I: Becoming-Sexual of the Sexual :: 1

II: Sound, Music, and Schizo-Incest :: 21

III: Clinical and Critical Perversion :: 43

References :: 67

About the Author :: 71

to Flutisttr

We must model ourselves an affirmative Idea of the Zero.

Jean-François Lyotard, *Libidinal Economy*

Foreword: The Undecidable

Manola Antonioli

Reading Deleuze like a musician, interested in philosophical rhythms, Zafer Aracagök draws our attention to the question of the "indécidable" in Deleuzian thought. His meeting with Deleuze and Guattari is obviously a "love affair," not a "business affair," nor is his task that of a professional philosopher who prepares his courses and makes profit out of his knowledge. Deleuze and Guattari's philosophy of becoming ("becoming-woman," "becoming-animal," "becoming-imperceptible," "becoming-intense," etc.) opens a crack in their thought which Aracagök pushes to its borders and extremes: as the lava of this volcanic thought flows out, "lines of flight," or the "witch's flight"—which both Deleuze and Guattari engineered in their common work—fracture into new combinations and consequences. The purpose of this operation is to bring to the foreground, by means of quantum theory as well as queer theory and psychonalysis, the aspects of Deleuze and Guattari's thought which remain implicit, dark, or always *indécidables*, even for the philosophers themselves. It is thus a question of repeating with Deleuze and Guattari what Deleuze proposed with the classical philosophers whom he studied (Spinoza, Kant, Leibniz, Nietzsche, Bergson): *to take them from behind.*

The undecidable could be here another name of what, in a very different tradition of thought, Jacques Derrida calls the *aporia*, from Greek *a-poros*, which means what is without outcome, without an already drawn path. "Becoming is real," and thus it's impossible to choose between the decidable and the undecidable: the decidable *is* undecidable. If Deleuze and Guattari recognize the becoming-woman of the woman and the becoming-woman of the man, they nevertheless hesitate in front of the becoming-man of the man or the multiple Nietzschean masks of the transvestite. Less radical or less quantum than Derrida, they hesitate at the edge of the volcano in eruption; they avoid thinking "becoming-queer" or "becoming-sexual of the sexual" without any synthesis; they avoid thinking the *aporia* of the undecidable, which is the task Aracagök takes up here in the first chapter of this small book.

Aracagök then takes up this question: Sound, noise and music—how can we decide among three? How can we browse the subterranean paths which separate them while also re-connecting them? One possible route by which to undertake this labor, Aracagök suggests, is to read Deleuze and Guattari reading Kafka, with Kafka's becoming-animal—his screams transformed into voices, and voices metamorphosing imperceptibly towards the scream, all of which offers us a line of flight for thinking this strange topology of a "non-relational relationship" between sonouros elements or sonouros events. If Deleuze in *The Logic of Sense* again seems to believe that there is a clear border between noise, sound, and voice, Aracagök, deterritorializing this border, re-deterritorializes the deterritorializing force of the sound that Deleuze and Guattari introduce in *Kafka: Towards a Minor Litterature* in order to establish a link between "schizo-incest" and sound: once more, the distinction between the audible and the inaudible is an undecidable one, which we can call, with the author, the "meta-audible."

In "Clinical and Critical Perversion," Büchner's unfinished 1836 novella *Lenz* becomes the exemplary test case of the undecidable which is simultaneously literary, political, psychoanalytical, and sexual, staged by the Body without Organs (BwO). It's a matter of an impossible *decision* between mimesis and diegesis, criticism and clinical practice, oedipal-incest and schizo-incest, psychastenia and schizophrenia—a strange topology where it is impossible to separate the traveller from the landscape (reminiscent of Nietzsche, for whom it was impossible to separate "big health" from illness). But *Lenz* also becomes a tool, for Aracagök, with which to think through the tradition of the notion of "perversion," as well as the undecidable position between man and animal, which may be one of the main sources of all undecidable matters. *Lenz* opens up a universe where, in Aracagök' words, "one no longer knows where one is," where one no longer knows *what one hears*, or with whom (man, woman, transvestite, or animal) s/he/it makes love.

"Becoming-sexual of the sexual," "schizo-incest," "meta-audible," "homosexual effusion," "critical perversion"—all may be "monstrous" concepts, which academic philosophy can never render completely familiar, but they are also, maybe, the (*undecidable*) concepts of the future :

> The future is necessarily monstrous: the figure of the future, that is, that which can only be surprising, that for which we are not prepared . . . is heralded by species of monsters. A future that would not be monstrous would not be a future; it would already be a predictable, calculable, and programmable tomorrow. All experience open to the future is prepared or prepares itself to welcome the monstrous arrivant.[1]

---

[1] Jacques Derrida, "Passages—from Truamatism to Promise," trans. Peggy Kamuf, in Jacques Derrida, *Points...: Interviews, 1976-1994*, ed. Elisabeth Weber (Stanford : Stanford University Press, 1995), 386–387 [372–395].

I: Becoming-Sexual of the Sexual[1]

> Or should we go a short way further to see for ourselves, be a little alcoholic, a little crazy, a little suicidal, a little of a guerilla—just enough to extend the crack, but not enough to deepen it irremediably?
>
> Gilles Deleuze, *The Logic of Sense*

0. VOLCANO

In a chapter called "Porcelain and Volcano"[2] in *The Logic of*

---

[1] A different and shorter version of this chapter was presented in 2007 at the opening of Phag-Off's Queer Jubilee in Rome, Italy, and was published as "Divenire sessuale dell'identitá sessuale," *Liberazione*, April 8, 2007. A revised and larger version appeared as "Cinsel-Oluş," in *Sanat ve Arzu Seminerleri*, eds. A. Özgün, Y. Madra, and A.O. Gültekin (Istanbul: Turkey, 2010), 65–79. The French version appeared as "Pour un principe d'incertitude sexuel(le)," *Revue Chimères* 73 (2010): 79–90. This version was initially published in *Rhizomes* 17 (Winter 2008): http://www.rhizomes.net/issue17/aracagok.html.

Sense, Deleuze describes a crack underneath of which there's a volcano ready to erupt at any moment. Considering this crack and also what he confessed in an interview as his practice of philosophising—that is, taking the philosophers he reads from behind[3]—I would like to introduce some preliminary concerns of this chapter's further expositions.

Reading Deleuze, for me, is a practice which requires a certain care on various levels simultaneously if one is not to reach reductionist conclusions in response to questions such as: What is immanence? What is becoming? What is a plane of consistency? What is becoming-woman? What is a concept? What is a Body Without Organs (BwO)? Et cetera. Despite the fact that Deleuze problematizes such answer-question dialectics, there is still a critical insistence on a certain appropriation, disappropriation, or misappropriation of Deleuzian thought which often eliminates, or elides, the question of the "undecidable." What is less certain or undecidable is whether, when Deleuze writes on other philosophers, he appropriates or disappropriates them by means of producing a critique of the philosophers in question. At such a juncture, it is quite appropriate to ask whether Deleuze identifies with, or properly appropriates, the philosopher he is taking from behind, so that his desire is quenched at the moment of satisfaction, or whether he continues producing desire so that his liaison with another philosopher will turn into a courtly love affair where both obedience and betrayal will be out of the question, either because an actual meeting will simply never

---

[2] Gilles Deleuze, *The Logic of Sense*, ed. Constantin Boundas, trans. Mark Lester and Charles Stivale (London: Continuum, 2003), 154–161.

[3] Actually, Deleuze says the following: "I saw myself as taking an author from behind and giving him a child that would be his own offspring, yet monstrous. It was really important for it to be his own child, because the author had to actually say all I had him saying": Gilles Deleuze, "Letter to a Harsh Critic," in Gilles Deleuze, *Negotiations*, trans. Martin Joughin (New York: Columbia University Press, 1995), 6.

occur or will always remain as an *event*.

The same applies to my affair with Deleuze and Guattari. Without generating loyalty to either of them, what I will offer here is to take two philosophers, Deleuze and Guattari, from behind in order to lay bare both mine and their unquenched desire with respect to the volcano which may erupt at any moment, thereby extending the crack to unfore-seen dimensions. To achieve the latter, I will first force this volcano to an eruption following some traces in the history and philosophy of quantum mechanics and what is theorized as "complementarity" by Niels Bohr and Arkady Plotnitsky. Can one produce the undecidable between the decidable and the undecidable in a tracing of the concept of "complementarity" in the philosophy of Deleuze and Guattari? Given this position, with respect to philosophy, I will seek to show that what is presented by Deleuze and Guattari as "becoming-woman" is a rather problematic issue which they put forward with a certain degree of undecidability and which, therefore, encapsulates other becomings (albeit in a cryptic form), the most important of which is becoming-queer, or rather, becoming-sexual of the sexual.

1. Quantum Theory

Quantum mechanics presents us with a productive background for explicating some points that remain obscure, undecidable, or even neglected by Deleuze and Guattari. I am thinking in particular of what I have mentioned as the undecidable, or undecidability—not simply in their texts, but also in the ways the terms are employed more widely. Most of the time these appear as something which could be decided, or as something which has already been decided, although they are passed off as something undecidable. I may be inviting judgements of paranoia in turning to quantum mechanics in connection with desire and the sexual. As we will see towards the end of this chapter, however, it is perhaps Deleuze and Guattari who get paranoid when it comes to the question of becoming, and especially to the question of becoming-woman. In contrast, I am writing here with no finality, without worrying about becoming paranoid, or even of getting hysterical.

It was as early as 1900 when quantum physics shook almost all the foundations of classical physics with a claim by Max Planck that radiation, such as light—previously believed to be a continuous phenomenon in all circumstances—can, under certain conditions, have a quantum or discontinuous character.[4] According to the classical view, light behaved as waves; however, in the years to come, especially after Einstein's discovery that light behaved like particles under certain circumstances, the classical view was brought face to face with the impossibility of observing the wave-like and particle-like character of light at the same time: something which did not allow for any visualisation or representation of the quantum phenomena in a proper single picture. It was right here, at this point, that the concept of "complementarity," as it was coined by Bohr, would be used to explain this mutual exclusivity (in a fashion similar to a Derridaean maneuver of maintaining opposites at the same time), which would come to designate Bohr's overall interpretation of quantum mechanics and from there, a general philosophical conceptuality.

If the main question was how one object could have such opposite characteristics—wave-like at one time and particle-like at another—further experiments bore witness to another realisation that "wave-like" and "particle-like" were not even attributes that should be ascribed to quantum objects, because these designations depended on classical concepts to explain radically new phenomena. In other words, these new designations brought along questions as to whether quantum objects could be thought of as "objects"[5] at all. Thus, classical

---

[4] Arkady Plotnitsky, *The Knowable and the Unknowable* (Ann Arbor: University of Michigan Press, 2002), 30.
[5] "For example, it may not be, and in Bohr's interpretation is not, possible to assign the standard attributes of the objects and motions of classical physics to the ultimate objects of quantum physics. It may no longer be possible to speak of objects or motions (such as part-

physics was brought as if face to face with the "unknowable," which is observable or visible only in its effects. The unknowable objects of quantum phenomena were considered to be "efficacities," which were accessible to us only through effects that could only be observed (and understood) within the concepts of classical physics.

The situation was like that of Kafka's dog in his story "The Investigations of a Dog," with the question: "'Whence does the Earth procure its food?" The food usually comes from above. Sometimes it hangs in the air, and sometimes the food even runs after the dog, but still the source that produces the food remains invisible. After the discovery of quantum discontinuity, it might be said that we have all become an Investigator dog. The fact that the dog in the story cannot see the source beyond the food points to a radical break between cause and effect, and its decision to fast, to be weightless, to float in the air (like the food or the soaring dogs in the story) points to the opacity of quantum objects that become visible only in their effects. If it wants to get to the source, the dog is left with no choice other than identifying with those weightless objects and with dogs floating in the air. Is this source attainable? Does becoming make us capable of reaching the source? Does the becoming-man of a dog make the dog capable of seeing the source? Only if we could picture a model—the model of the model which is, however, unknowable. Hence, classical physics was in real trouble; working on the principle of causality, classical physics required, first and foremost, the construction of a model according to which the interaction between natural objects and natural phenomena could be observed, measured, theorised, explained, and verified. However, in quantum mechanics, since only the interaction between the effects of the efficacities and the measuring instruments could be described, it did not allow for a construction of such a model.

As Bohr put it, all this required a renunciation or a revis-

---

icles, or waves, for example), which, however, does not imply that nothing exists or everything stands still" (Plotnitsky 2002: 3).

ion of not only causality and visualisation, but also, "our attitude towards the problem of physical reality."[6] If the unknowable was "knowable" only through its effects—that is, through the concepts of classical physics—then such a situation also required a revision of what constituted this "reality" which hardly obeyed the model of a model, or, rather, the concept of a model according to classical physics. Imagine Artaud's neurotic language, or Mallarmé's crypt—singularities of representation which do not follow any order—or Nietzsche's dream of getting rid of grammar. In contrast to classical, causal, and deterministic ways of constructing models according to models, quantum phenomena proved that such a concept of a model did not properly work because in quantum mechanics, that which was taken for granted—physical reality *as such*—was at stake. Consequently, if such a presumption could not be produced, then, without doubt, the construction of a model, even the construction of a model of a model, would fail. The situation was like being in a Merzbow concert where you are in front of a wall of sound, and the sonics you hear give you only some clues about what lies behind this wall; given that Merzbow does not imitate what he cannot hear but even short-circuits the act of hearing, he questions our capacity to hear the things at the heart of hearing and his failure in representing them.[7]

This approach to "physical reality" foregrounded Bohr's concept of complementarity and his approach to models and copies, or rather to the question of mimesis that this concept encapsulates. From this angle, quantum theory can be seen as a crisis in representation, models, and mimesis which raised doubts about classical methods—the "Platonic" model of a model—by way of which science in general had been capable of representing phenomena as "reasonable." With the rise of quantum phenomena, what is put at stake is the visibility of such phenomena, and hence their representability. In this

---

[6] Plotnitsky 2002: 42.
[7] Merzbow is the stage name of avant-garde Japanese noise musician Masami Akita (b. 1956).

sense, Bohr is no Hegelian, and his concept of complementarity thus also puts at risk the Hegelian notion of "synthesis." The position raised by Bohr assumes the form of a critique of—as we know it from Derrida—a "metaphysics of presence." Considering all these characteristics, it was as if Bohr was underlining a deconstructionist strategy where one cannot produce a synthesis unless one takes the metaphysics of presence for granted. For Bohr, what took the place of synthesis was a concern for this rupture: the abyss.

Bohr can perhaps be considered as a Bataille of the world of physics—a non-Hegelian Hegelian who disrupts any kind of synthesis between opposites, forcing an understanding of the limits without synthesis, yet also pushing them forward to widen the crack, to make it deeper, still knowing by not knowing where to stop. Or, he is Büchner's Lenz[8] five minutes before he starts hearing the noise of silence, or goes mad, or attempts to kill himself. In contrast, a thorough understanding of complementarity means to look at killing oneself together with the impossibility of killing oneself, thus extending the rumination of complementarity to a life-long project.

2. BECOMING –

Where should we seek the traces of the concept of complementarity in the philosophy of Deleuze and Guattari which point to the yawning crack, the complementarity of the decidable and the undecidable in their theory? Their concept of the rhizome may offer us a good opening, but it will also be too simple an opening, immediately giving us the opportunity for identification. As we said before, our intention is to extend the crack and look at the volcano (risking eruption)—the non-identifiable, the non-identitarian, the undecidable, or better, the unnegotiable—in the face. For all these reasons, and

---

[8] See Georg Büchner, *Lenz*, in Georg Büchner, *Complete Works and Letters*, trans. Henry J. Schmidt (New York: Continuum, 1991), 139–162. I will return to this unfinished novella, originally published in 1836, in Chap. 3 of this volume.

perhaps with the intention of becoming-becoming itself, I'd rather concentrate especially on a particular chapter of Deleuze and Guattari's *A Thousand Plateaus*, namely, "1730: Becoming-Intense, Becoming-Animal, Becoming-Imperceptible ...".

The whole chapter about "becoming" can be read as being based on a presumed opposition between what Deleuze and Guattari call the "plane of consistency" and the "plane of organisation." If the plane of consistency should be understood as a plane where there are no given forms, subjects, structure, or genesis, and where unformed elements, molecules, or any type of particles are related to each other only by means of speed and movement, the plane of organisation is its opposite in the sense that here we have structure and genesis, which, remaining hidden behind things, produce forms, subjects, and organisations. In other words, the plane of organisation is a transcendental plane, the constitutive principle of which lies outside itself, whereas the plane of consistency is an immanent one which does not refer to such an outside—to a transcendental principle—in order to produce forms, structures, or organisation as in a mimetic relationship between a model and a copy.

According to Deleuze and Guattari, our understanding of nature (and therefore our understanding of animals and ourselves) is determined by two distinct approaches—one of series and the other of structures—but both of them are based on a mimetic vision. Although these approaches seem to be different from each other, in both of them, beings develop by imitating one another on the basis of an originary model, and, therefore, in the end, both boil down to the same plane of organisation. In the serial approach, one proceeds in a linear fashion by resemblances, and, in the other, by means of structural analogies.

It is actually in contrast to these approaches, or rather against the determining mimetic factor in each, that Deleuze and Guattari offer their concept of becoming. As they put it, "a becoming is not a correspondence between relations. But neither is it a resemblance, an imitation, or, at the limit, an identification."[9] Moreover, becoming (or rather, the becoming-animal) is real. The reality of such a becoming is not due to the fact that the one who becomes animal imitates the animal, but rather due to that which becomes real being becoming itself. If becoming is the principle of the plane of consistency where there are no forms, subjects, or organisations, then becoming cannot have a subject or, as they put it, "produces nothing other than itself."[10] Kafka's dog never becomes the food that it wants to become, but perhaps it enacts at least the becoming-food of a dog. As Deleuze and Guattari claim:

> This is the point to clarify: that a becoming lacks a subject distinct from itself; but also that it has no term, since its term in turn exists only as taken up in another becoming of which it is the subject, and which coexists, forms a block, with the first. This is the principle according to which there is a reality specific to becoming.
>
> ...
>
> Becoming is certainly not imitating, or identifying with something; neither is it regressing-progressing; neither is it corresponding, establishing corresponding relations; neither is it producing, producing a filiation or producing through filiation.[11]

Becoming-animal, in that sense, is to recognize the multiplicity in animals and the packs they form against the serial or structural understandings of nature where they are constituted as individuals by means of reducing the differences between species, or between members of species, to the same. The rhizomic constitution of these packs—their multiplicity—

---

[9] Gilles Deleuze and Félix Guattari, *A Thousand Plateaus*, trans. Brian Massumi (Minneapolis: University of Minnesota Press, 1987), 237–348.
[10] Deleuze and Guattari 1987: 238.
[11] Deleuze and Guattari 1987: 238, 239.

does not let becoming-multiple or becoming-animal processes be self-identical or mimetic; on the contrary, it produces a "fascination for the outside"[12] where the boundaries encompassing subjects and forms are opened up to various multiplicities. This is actually what the famous psychoanalytic case Wolfman illustrates: the call of the wolves in his dream is a call for embracing multiplicities.

On the other hand, for Deleuze and Guattari, multiplicities cannot be defined by the elements that compose them, but by their lines and dimensions which are momentarily countable due to their borderlines.[13] In other words, it means we can define multiplicities by the number of their dimensions. Yet, doesn't this definition invite a certain danger that is the constitution of certain "forms," specifically "forms" of different multiplicities by way of reduction (a practice which is in contradiction with the definition of plane of consistency)? As they note this danger, Deleuze and Guattari take precautions against it:

> If multiplicities are defined and transformed by the borderline that determines in each instance their number of dimensions, we can conceive of the possibility of laying them out on a plane, the borderlines succeeding one another, forming a broken line. It is only in appearance that a plane of this kind "reduces" the number of dimensions; for it gathers in all the dimensions to the extent that flat multiplicities—which nonetheless have an increasing or decreasing number of dimensions—are inscribed upon it.[14]

What is said or reformulated here in the face of the "dangers" is actually to present the question of form as if it were

---

[12] Deleuze and Guattari 1987: 240.

[13] "A multiplicity is defined not by its elements, nor by a centre of unification or comprehension. It is defined by the number of dimensions it has; it is not divisible, it cannot lose or gain a dimension without changing its nature" (Deleuze and Guattari 1987: 249).

[14] Deleuze and Guattari 1987: 251.

composed of "broken lines" or as a reduction "only in appearance," which is not the same as the concept of form produced on the plane of organisation. Is this possible? Let us be patient, however, before we decide that even this type of formulation requires a mimetic relationship between a model and a copy. In other words, let's see if talking about form not as form but as "broken lines" can save any discussion from yielding to form, and from the necessity of models and copies.

Right after this discussion, Deleuze and Guattari introduce two sections one after another, entitled "Memories of a Spinozist, I" and "Memories of a Spinozist, II," as if to support their points about the immanence of this plane with reference to Spinoza. If becoming-animal is the first step in their theory of "becoming," it is solely because becoming-animal produces good grounds for the theorisation of an "absolute" plane of consistency and a proper passage for man from a static state of being to becoming. Becoming-animal, under the light of dense references to Spinoza, becomes a total immersion into a disorganisation of the body where that body meets its Body without Organs (BwO). As we know it from other sources, the BwO for Deleuze and Guattari is that which knows no boundaries as to the organisation of the body, and is a total rejection of the bounded body's organs and functions. If organisation, as in the case of psychoanalysis (which "killed becoming-animal, in the adult as in the child"[15]), concerns the mimetic in an Oedipal triangle, composition means starting from a zero point where there are no models to imitate.

After these two rigorous sections on Spinoza, it looks as if the crack which was about to yield to a disaster has thus been prevented, and that which has been left suspended as an undecidable has been restored as decidable again by asserting the plane of consistency as an absolute. Now it seems as if Merzbow can continue producing noise, but we should prefer so-called sound artists, or Kim Cascone, as the artists of the world of immediacy.[16] However, things become complicated

---

[15] Deleuze and Guattari 1987: 259.
[16] Kim Cascone (b. 1955) is an American composer of ambient music.

and eventually confused in the section that follows this decision. As if all the discussion about the absoluteness of the plane of consistency is undertaken in vain, here, in "Memories of a Plan(e) Maker," we observe Deleuze and Guattari claiming the necessity of the plane of organisation as a counterforce in opposition to the plane of consistency. Now the crack is opened up again, as if the earlier necessity for a model, right before they are to theorise becoming-woman, gets urgent, and they say, "Perhaps there are two planes, or two ways of conceptualising the plane."[17] And after they define the planes of consistency and organisation, they decide to put them into an opposition, as follows:

> one continually passes from one to the other, by unnoticeable degrees and without being aware of it, or one becomes aware of it only afterwards. Because one continually reconstitutes one plane atop other, or extricates one from the other. For example, all we need to do is to sink the floating plane of immanence, bury it in the depths of Nature instead of allowing it to play freely on the surface, for it to pass to the other side and assume the role of a ground that can no longer be anything more than a principle of analogy from the standpoint of organisation, and a law of continuity from the standpoint of development.[18]

One wonders: what happened to the "absolute" plane of consistency? And why is this a two-way passage now? One thing for sure is that the way they formulate this relationship is a warning that we should not see it as a Hegelian relationship; that is, it is not a dialectical one, but rather it has some affinities with a Bataillian relationship between a general and restricted economy, or, shall we say, complementarity. Yet even so, one still wonders if one of these planes play the role of a ground for the other—of which Deleuze in *Difference*

---

[17] Deleuze and Guattari 1987: 265.
[18] Deleuze and Guattari 1987: 269–270.

and Repetition was severely critical. At this point, perhaps we should remember Bataille's reading of Hegel: the moves by means of which he eliminated the synthesis from Hegel, and thus unravelled his thought of transgression. Can we say that a similar thing is happening here, leading any synthesis between general and restricted economy to an impossibility? Can we say that this relationship between two planes is not mimetic? Moreover, should we suspect that these two planes are put into a relationship of a model and a copy? Will the investigations of a dog reach a telos? Before deciding about these matters, let us see how Deleuze and Guattari theorise "becoming-woman," which I believe will throw light on these issues and open up for us a way to theorize "becoming-queer," or "becoming-sexual of the sexual," without any synthesis, and thus move towards a transgression, or an impossibility based on a complementarity of the planes of consistency and of organisation.

According to Deleuze and Guattari, the distinction between molecular and molar is layered onto either a rejection or acceptance of imitation on the basis of a pre-existing model. Becoming-animal, becoming-child, and becoming-woman are molecular becomings because they are not based on imitating such a model. If, therefore, woman, as defined by a certain form with organs and functions assigned to a certain subject, is a molar entity, becoming-woman is molecular because what it requires is not imitation.[19] Becoming-woman is rather "emitting particles that enter the relations of movement and rest, or the zone of proximity, of a microfemininity, in other words, that produce in us a molecular woman, create the molecular woman."[20] But, in the meantime, right in between these two quotations, they also add: "We are not, however, overlooking the importance of imitation, or moments of

---

[19] "What we term a molar entity is, for example, the woman as defined by her form, endowed with organs and functions and assigned as a subject. Becoming woman is not imitating this entity or even transforming oneself into it" (Deleuze and Guattari 1987: 275).
[20] Deleuze and Guattari 1987: 275.

imitation among certain homosexual males, much less the prodigious attempt at a real transformation on the part of certain transvestites."[21] Strangely enough, although the transformation of the transvestite in question (that they accept and promise not to overlook) is based on imitation, its importance (or its difference) gets lost in the text and does not reappear. It is actually in relationship to this not reappearing that I would like to raise the following questions: Do they think that the transvestite imitates the "woman" and thus fails to get into the process of becoming-woman? Or, is the imitation assumed by the transvestite of a different order: a mimetic one without a model? However, in both cases, how do we know that the transvestite is imitating a woman, and where is this woman, and why doesn't she appear *as such*?

To produce answers to these questions, and also to force that volcanic crack to widen, getting deeper down into the abyss, we should also consider becoming-woman on the basis of the relationship between the plane of consistency and the plane of organisation. If, as Deleuze and Guattari say, the body is stolen from us "to fabricate opposable organisms,"[22] it results from the preponderance of the plane of organisation over the plane of consistency. The form that we know as, and is signified by the term, "woman," is constituted by the "man's" stealing the girl's becoming from her,[23] and it is in that sense that the girl constitutes the first sex from whom things are stolen in order to model her in accordance with the male order upon a certain plane of organisation. Becoming-woman in this framework connotes a deterritorialisation from the plane of organisation to the plane of consistency, which is

---

[21] Deleuze and Guattari 1987: 275.
[22] "The question is fundamentally that of the body—the body they *steal* from us in order to fabricate opposable organisms. The body is stolen first from the girl ... . The girl's becoming is stolen first, in order to impose a history, or prehistory, upon her. The boy's turn comes next, but it is by using the girl as an example, by pointing to the girl as the object of his desire, that an opposed history, a dominant history is fabricated for him" (Deleuze and Guattari 1987: 276).
[23] Deleuze and Guattari 1987: 276.

not based on any model. In other words, if the plane of consistency is the body without organs, the plane of organisation is the male organising principle, which, stealing from the girl her becoming, also constitutes itself as "man." And, since the identity of this thief is determined by Deleuze and Guattari as "man," there is no becoming-man for "man." They support their view by claiming that "'man' constituted a standard in the universe in relation to which men necessarily (analytically) form a majority."[24] Well, everything is fine here insofar as we are satisfied with an analytical determination of the majority as male. Or, in other words, let us pretend that, as the male majority that has supposedly accepted being man as a given fact, we all represent Franco Nero of Fassbinder's *Querelle*.

However, if we don't accept it, and moreover, if we reject such a position (as, for example, a clinical pervert who draws cocks on the walls as if to amplify his masochistic pleasure, his failure to celebrate his success of not-yet-being-a-"man"), and if we are still curious about this thief, we can still ask: doesn't this thief who steals from the girl her becoming also steal his becoming from the boy? And moreover, we can still ask: Who is this thief? And where is he? Don't Deleuze and Guattari presume here that "man" has completed his becoming-man not only as a statistical determination but also as a sexual becoming, a becoming-sexual?

With these questions in mind, my aim is to shift the argument from analytical or statistical determination, by means of which Deleuze and Guattari reserve no becoming-man to "man," to the question of sexual difference, which concerns two basic sexes: simply, man and woman. Man, analytically or statistically, might have repressed women and stolen her becoming from her, but there are also things stolen from boys so as to constitute man *as such* as an analytical majority. I believe the identity of this thief—if there is one—can be used to answer our questions which have been proliferating in different directions in something of a hysterical

---

[24] Deleuze and Guattari 1987: 291.

fashion.

First of all, as we have seen throughout my exposition here, Deleuze and Guattari invite the thought of an opposing plane to the plane of consistency only after they are alarmed by the impossibility of talking about form without a model. The plane of consistency, as they discuss it, constitutes a ground for the interaction between two planes; however, its nature should be thought of not as a model preceding the forms that appear on the plane of organisation, but rather as an image of thought which has no determining power. The difficulty of such a way of thinking, however—as I explained it elsewhere[25]—is not only theirs, but also the flaw of thought in general: to think without Hegel, or to be able to think without turning the whole theory into a restricted economy. Actually, as we have witnessed before in Deleuze and Guattari, all emanates from our inability to conceive such a formless plane—an undifferentiated one—without considering something that precedes it as its model. And the plane of consistency—much against their theorisation—turns into a model for plane of organisation, as I outline below.

Let's go back to the discussion where "man" potentially becomes the "thief." As they argue, man steals from the girl her becoming, and in this framework, the girl is the first from whom becoming has been stolen. One of the most serious deductions we can draw from this moment in their text is that, in such a moment of stealing, Deleuze and Guattari presume that man *as such* has always already been formed. In other words, man, having always already been formed *as such* and at the same time constituting the plane of organisation according to a male principle, steals girl's becoming from her. But, at the moment of this stealing, there is also another thing that happens; if the man is always already formed as "man," he without doubt owes it to the plane of consistency which he must have used as his model, as his rigid model of man (despite the apparent contradiction that the plane of consistency,

---

[25] See my article "Decalcomania, Mapping and Mimesis," *Symploke* 13.1-2 (2006): 283–302.

according to their theory, cannot be used as a model and is formless). This must be so, otherwise man's coming into being as man cannot be explained—that is, without referring to a model. Despite this apparent contradiction, Deleuze and Guattari still insist on not giving the same quality to man so that he can also be seen in a becoming just as in becoming-woman. Moreover, when and how has man become man? For me, the main reason why Deleuze and Guattari cannot give man this quality is because no matter how they insist on not having a model-copy relationship between the planes, there is actually a model-copy relationship between the two, and becoming-woman also obeys this determination, at the end of which both women and men will analytically be equalised. If the nature of imitation of the transvestite does not reappear in their text, it is mainly because of this contradiction, which, if taken seriously, would reveal the fact that the becoming they are speaking of (by not speaking of it) is actually based on a mimetic order where both man and woman imitate something, something like a model which cannot be known *as such*. And if there's a thief in this sense, this thief becomes a thief not only by stealing from the girl her becoming but also by the boy's becoming, because he—as it were, with a capital H—is blinded by sexual difference, which shouldn't be reduced according to an analytical determination.[26]

---

[26] On another level, things can be summed up as follows: initially, it seems like the plane of consistency—since it is a "ground"—is offered by Deleuze and Guattari as an unbounded or infinite model on which plane of organisation organises forms and subjects. And, since the model is infinite, it doesn't determine the forms as absolutes. However, on a second look, we can see, as we have seen before, how the multiplicities constituted on plane of consistency—although this is a plane of the undifferentiated—are determined by means of their numbers of dimension. It is actually this momentary reconciliation of shape and form (a la Leibniz) which puts forward the plane of consistency as an infinitely finite model acting behind the plane of organisation. Therefore, much against their critique formerly of the plane of organisation which, as they say, is based on a transcendental principle, the latter also becomes the principle of their theory where

It is with reference to this theorisation that I will also claim that what is called becoming-woman in Deleuze and Guattari is always already determined even before one gets into the process of becoming-woman, stolen first by the male order, and then by this transcendental which never totally disappears from their discourse—the discourse that, much against their efforts, fails to preserve it as "undecidable." That is, the analytically obtained preponderance of man over woman cannot be obtained so easily when it comes to sexual difference because the analytical—as it does most of the time—blinds us to sexual difference, which can neither be so easily appropriated nor disappropriated. It is at this point I am offering to widen and deepen the volcanic crack so that the undecidability between the sexes becomes more visible; there is a certain crack between man and woman as far as the sexual difference between man and woman is concerned, yet that they are different means that neither does each sex originates from an essence—neither of them has an ultimate telos, except perhaps that of being in a continuous becoming, a becoming-sexual of the sexual. And again, if the question of the transvestite doesn't reappear in the text, it is because s/he forces this undecidability to such an extremity that the absence of any essence or telos becomes destructive, even putting at risk any attempt at theorisation.

Let us imagine a complementary relationship between becoming-man and becoming-woman:

- where both boy's and girl's becomings never become what they are … ; and,
- where "man" and "woman" will be conceived as the effects of unknowable efficacities … just as the radicality of the transvestite's becoming-transvestite.

Should we call this plane the plane of becoming-queer? Or

---

plane of consistency is turned into a transcendental behind the plane of organisation.

will it still be much too деterministic, given the fact that we are not talking about finite models? But does becoming-queer also mean to talk about finite models? One wonders ...

Wouldn't calling it a plane of becoming-queer turn it into an impossible project, given the unknowability of what "woman" and "man" are?

At this point, perhaps we can think of another name for this plane: the plane of becoming-sexual of the sexual where that which is hidden behind the forms, behind "man" and "woman," behind sexual difference, will never yield itself as a model ... but the difference will be the condition of continuous becomings—that is, sexually.

And what is the name for this plane where the undecidable can be preserved as undecidable? (Not because it is a defensible project, but as an impossible project, one that is always imperceptible.)

II: Sound, Music, and Schizo-Incest[1]

0. META-AUDIBLE

Deleuze and Guattari's *Kafka: Towards a Minor Literature* still continues throwing threads, or threats, of deterritorialisation—some tangled, some rooted, and some uprooted or flattened. What is most striking in this atypical topology of links is not what upsets a certain notion of topology, but rather some subterrennean pathways which, especially in the Kafka book, lead to an enigmatic approach to the question of the aural that disappears at the moment of what it purports to be proposing. Namely, I am thinking of a possible relationship

---

[1] This article was formerly published as "Deleuze on Sound, Music, and Schizo-Incest," in *Rhizomes* 19 (Summer 2009): http://www.rhizomes.net/issue19/aracagok.html. The Spanish version appeared as "Deleuze: Sobre el Sonido, la Música y el Esquizo-Incesto," in *Hacer audibles ... Devenires, Planos y Afecciones Sonoras entre Deleuze y la Música Contemporánea*, eds. Santiago Diaz and Juan Pablo Sosa (Argentine: Universidad Nacional de Mar del Plata, 2013), 79-98. The Turkish version was published as "Deleuze: Ses, Müzik ve Şizo-Ensest Üzerine," *Göçebe Düşünmek* (Metis, Istanbul) (December 2014): 319-337.

between sound, noise, and music, or the audible in general, and the question of schizo-incest which, coming up much later in the Kafka book, is not put into a resonance with the idea of the audible. Perhaps these threads should never be linked, questioned, nor put into resonance, yet the reason why I insist on offering a relationship between the two (schizo-incest and the audible) is simply because, whether or not they can be taken as a model (a model of a non-relational relationship) has implications not only for a different line of flight, but also for an explanation of how Deleuzian-Guattarian concepts can lead entwined lives of their own without any necessity of a link. To obtain such a model when we have been talking about enigmas and missing links is, without doubt, a contradiction in terms; however, since both sound and schizo-incest are related to the question of form, and the link between the two is, I believe, an elusive one, they can also be taken as bearing witness to an enigmatic model which is not a model at all.

For all those concerns above, in this chapter, I will first problematise Deleuze's formulation of a certain passage from "noise to voice," and his approach to "distance," in *The Logic of Sense*, if only to be able to throw light on what baffles us in Deleuze and Guatarri's reading of Kafka's "The Investigations of a Dog." In their reading, sound, when deterritorialized, is a formless element that is still audible, much like the aural experiences in Kafka's other stories, especially in "Josephine The Singer, or the Mouse Folk" and "The Silence of the Sirens," where the audience is often said to have heard something, yet the knowledge of what is heard is suspended. Yet such a suspension, I shall argue, leads us to a different knowledge—that is, the realm of the "formless" or the "unformed," which cannot be obtained without destroying what we know of as "hearing" or the "audible."

One of the guiding questions here therefore will be whether the formless can be heard or recognised as sound within the framework of the audible. Proposing in the end a limit experience, which I call the "meta-audible," I will try to show that Kafka's radicalising approach to sound creates a line of flight that escapes even from the line of flight itself. Moreover, such a flight, when brought into contact with the notion of self-shattering, provides the missing link, or rather, the resonance between the meta-audible and schizo-incest.

1. THE PASSAGE FROM NOISE TO VOICE

There's a strange passage in *The Logic of Sense*, under the guidance of which one passes not only from noise to voice but also from the unformed to the formed. I shall contextualize this passage briefly in order to foreground how "form" is maintained in Deleuzian philosophy in general.

Deleuze's formulation of the "individual" in *The Logic of Sense* is saturated with rigorous discussions on the relationship between series and the resonance between them, the constitution of events, the actualisation and counter-actualisation of the events, the disjunctive synthesis and its affirmation, etc., which eventually lead to "The Twenty-Fifth Series of Univocity." The latter functions as a way of opening up the concept of "individual" to all the compossible worlds, so that the "individual" will be organised within a multiplicity as an "event." In other words, this is purely a question of form— that is, how to transcend the question of the form, known as the "individual."[2] Such a transcendence, if it is possible, requires in the first place (as we know it from *Difference and Repetition*) radicalising the "image of thought" so that there will no more be a form on which the constitution of the individual (or of any concept) *as such* is based, and what is known as "individual" will be constituted on the basis of simulacrum—not on the basis of mimesis—and thus s/he will be freed from being shaped by any predetermined model. On the other hand, if such a project means to open up the in-

---

[2] "The problem is therefore one of knowing how the individual would be able to transcend his form and his syntactical link with world": Gilles Deleuze, *The Logic of Sense*, ed. Constantin Boundas, trans. Mark Lester and Charles Stivale (London: Continuum, 2003), 178.

dividual to multiplicities, it will also have to deal with the question of ontology, because even if Deleuze explains it by positing pre-individual singularities, they will nevertheless require an appearance, a moment of being, or, rather, a passage from absence to presence (or from non-being to being, if you like). Therefore, in "Univocity," Deleuze proposes:

> Philosophy merges with ontology, but ontology merges with the univocity of Being. ... The univocity of Being does not mean that there is one and the same Being; on the contrary, beings are multiple and different, they are always produced by a disjunctive synthesis, and they themselves are disjointed and divergent, *membra disjuncta*. The univocity of Being signifies that Being is Voice that it is said, and that it is said in one and the same "sense" of everything about which it is said. It occurs, therefore, as a unique event for everything that happens to the most diverse things, *Eventum tantum* for all events, the ultimate form of all the forms which remain disjointed in it, but which bring about the resonance and the ramification of their disjunction.[3]

In this passage, if univocity signifies an event—an event of all events—it also points to a concern for genesis, where "voice" can be rethought as a generic force, which makes genesis itself possible by triggering a passage between "that which comes before voice" and voice.

In the "Twenty-Sixth Series of Language," all the questions which have been actually gravitating towards the possibility of such a passage find the origin to which they have been pointing.[4] Therefore, Deleuze opens this series with a conviction

---

[3] Deleuze 2003: 179.

[4] In other words, if the discussions on sense and nonsense, paradoxical entity, and the event, up to the discussion on the univocity of being, were concerned with the relationship between the word and the thing, or the duality of eating/speaking and its displacement into the proposition—that is, into the duality of denotation and expression—it was because they have all been pointing to this passage

that "events make language possible,⁵ and he immediately adds,

> But making possible does not mean causing to begin. ... To render language possible thus signifies assuring that sounds are not confused with the sonorous qualities of things, with the sound effects of bodies, or with their actions and passions. What renders language possible is that which separates sounds from bodies and organizes them into propositions, freeing them for the expressive function. It is always a mouth which speaks, but the sound is no longer the noise of a body which eats—a pure orality—in order to become the manifestation of a subject expressing itself. ... And in truth, without the event all of this would be only noise—and an indistinct noise.⁶

And, in the next series, "Twenty-Seventh Series of Orality," he also adds, "We constantly relive in our dreams the passage from noise to voice."⁷

So, for Deleuze, there is such a thing as a moment of absolute separation: a passage, between sounds and sonorous elements (noise), made possible by the events. And events not only make possible the language, but also the subject. From now on, a decision which was present and suspended—probably due to the impossibility of saying something and its sense at the same time, but conversely, also due to the possibility of saying it, given the impossibility of escaping from representation—since the beginning of *The Logic of Sense* is thus given here an "appearance," and this also makes possible the history of the psyche, which Deleuze reconstructs by reading his own theory of the sense and the event into psychoanalysis (more specifically, into the works of Melanie

---

that would make possible a rigorous discussion on "language," which would also constitute an origin for "individual," and "psyche" in the rest of *The Logic of Sense*.
⁵ Deleuze 2003: 181.
⁶ Deleuze 2003: 181–182.
⁷ Deleuze 2003: 194.

Klein and Jacques Lacan).

Let's stop here and think about what might probably have led to such a passage from the unformed to the formed in Deleuze's work, not because it is thinkable or localisable with an exact clarity of thought, but because at least it can be shown without making appear what cannot appear. Looking back at the earlier "Twenty-Fourth Series," centered on "communication of the events," we find Deleuze celebrating Leibniz as the "first theoretician of the event," for it was Leibniz who saw for the first time that "'compossible' and 'incompossible' cannot be reduced to the identical and contradictory, which govern only the possible and the impossible."[8] If compossibility is defined, on a pre-individual level, by the convergence of the series, the incompossibility is defined by the divergence of the series. However, Leibniz made use of these definitions only to the extent that the compossible worlds, being incompossible with the best possible of all the worlds (our world), should therefore diverge from it. Hence, "He made a negative use of divergence of disjunction—one of exclusion."[9] So, Deleuze's critique of Leibniz is directed to the negative use of divergence by Leibniz, and therefore he is concerned with a Nietzschean affirmation of divergences where God, being dead, does not choose anymore the best possible world. Deleuze asks: "But what does it mean to make divergence and disjunction the objects of affirmation"?[10] Of course, it means the irreducibility of the difference to the same and identical:

> We are no longer faced with an identity of contraries, which would still be inseparable as such from a movement of the negative and of exclusion. We are rather faced with a positive distance of different elements: no longer to identify two contraries with the same, but to affirm their distance as that which relates one to the other insofar as

---

[8] Deleuze 2003: 171.
[9] Deleuze 2003: 172.
[10] Deleuze 2003: 172.

they are "different." The idea of a positive distance (and not as an annulled or overcome distance) appears to us essential, since it permits the measuring of contraries through their finite difference instead of equating difference with a measureless contrariety, and contrariety with an identity which is itself infinite. It is not difference which must "go as far as" contradiction, as Hegel thought in his desire to accommodate the negative; it is the contradiction which must reveal the nature of *its* difference as it follows the distance corresponding to it. The idea of positive distance belongs to topology and to the surface.[11]

The positive distance, therefore, is finite, but its finitude, instead of foregrounding a contradiction that can be overcome by means of a dialectical synthesis (which measure gains importance insofar as the distance can be overcome so that the contradiction can be resolved), puts forward distance as a situation where the difference between two things is preserved and made open to topological determination, so that it can appear and be measured. And thus we have Deleuze's illustration of the matter with Nietzsche's perspectivism, or his capacity to reverse certain perspectives: health in sickness and sickness in health, where the two states are not seen as contraries in a dialectical scheme, but as levers for preserving distance *as distance* (as a measurable distance between two states), not only in order to observe their convergence, but also their divergence, thus affirming their difference. So, having a perspective and a capacity to reverse it is a matter of the irreducibility of the two divergent elements as a result of which one gains a point of view, in Leibnizean fashion—not from the point of view of oneself, but from the point of view of things themselves. There is here only one radical difference from Leibniz, where one observes only the affirmation of those perspectives that converge, whereas in Nietzsche

the point of view is opened onto a divergence which it

---

[11] Deleuze 2003: 172–173.

affirms ... . Each term becomes the means of going all the way to the end of another, by following the entire distance. Nietzsche's perspective—his perspectivism—is a much more profound art than Leibniz's point of view, for divergence is no longer a principle of exclusion, a disjunction no longer a means of separation. Incompossibility is now a means of communication.[12]

One should also add that opening the point of view onto divergence erases the discontinuity between the possible and the incompossible, and therefore a maximum continuity is maintained not only between things in the most possible world, but also between all the worlds, whether possible and/or incompossible.

In the same paragraph, after celebrating Nietzsche's perspectivism on health and illness, Deleuze also comments on what happens to this perspectivism after Nietzsche goes mad:

Conversely, Nietzsche does not lose his health when he is sick, but when he can no longer affirm the distance, when he is no longer able, by means of his health, to establish sickness as a point of view on health (then, as the Stoics say, the role is over, the play has ended).[13]

There are possible conclusions to be maintained at the end of this detour on the question of "distance" in Deleuze. First and foremost, if "positive distance" is "affirmable," this means it is also topologically maintainable (though not determinable), and it will eventually have a moment of appearance, a moment of being "specular," just as in the case of a passage from "noise to voice," or from the unformed to the formed. However, here let us be reminded of what Nietzsche said in *The Gay Science* with respect to question of distance, throwing much light on the non-topological character of "distance" in his work, and thereby problematising any such passage from

---

[12] Deleuze 2003: 174.
[13] Deleuze 2003: 173.

the unformed to the formed:

> Not to be dead and yet no longer alive? ... It seems as if the noise here has led me into fantasies. All great noise leads us to move happiness into some quiet distance. When a man stands in the midst of his own noise, in the midst of his own surf of plans and projects, then he is apt also to see quiet, magical beings gliding past him and to long for their happiness and seclusion: women. He almost thinks that his better self dwells there among the women, and that in these quiet regions even the loudest surf turns into deathly quiet, and life itself into a dream about life. Yet! Yet! Noble enthusiast, even on the most beautiful sailboat there is a lot of noise, and unfortunately much small and petty noise. The magic and the most powerful effect of women is, in philosophical language, action at a distance, *actio in distans*; but this requires first of all and above all—distance.[14]

2. INVESTIGATIONS OF A DOG

At this juncture, I wonder about the possible relationships between Nietzsche's reference to "distance" and that of Kafka's dog in "The Investigations of a Dog." But let us first briefly summarise the story. Kafka's dog, when he was only a small puppy, experiences a strange encounter with some musician dogs, the traumatic nature of which becomes clear as the dog unfolds his story. One thing that is certain is that, in this encounter, he hears something that comes to him as a blast—a blast not only to his ears but also to his whole body, which shakes all of his being down to the ground. Overwhelmed by what he experiences, he shouts questions at the musician dogs; the lack of answers to his questions leads not only to an impossibility to find the words to explain what happened to him, but also to his way of being thereafter,

---

[14] Friedrich Nietzsche, *The Gay Science*, trans. Walter Kaufmann (New York: Vintage Books, 1974), Fragment 60, 123–124.

where he is dedicated to incessant investigations about almost everything. Oscillating between knowing and not knowing whether what he heard is music, the investigations of the dog in time gravitate to one focal question: "Whence does the earth procure its food"?[15]

Another issue that arises during his investigations is the matter of "soaring dogs," about which only some speculations are available. According to the rumour or to some observations, these creatures exist by doing nothing but resting in the air.[16] What concerns the Investigator dog in this instance is whether one becomes a soaring dog by propogation or by willing. Such ontological questions about various matters do not please the dog nation, so the more he asks, the more they fill his mouth with food.[17] Be that as it may, the silencing of his questions does not stop him from asking further questions, and the ensuing silence, as he comments later, is that place beyond which there exists an unbearable noise and the formless.

In the face of this silence, the Investigator dog goes back to his central question: "Whence does the earth procure its food?"[18] In order to prove that the food comes from the above, he decides not to receive any food from the ground, and to fast so that if it comes to his mouth and asks for admittance, it would be the proof of his theory. As he fasts, the sudden appearance of a hunter awakens him to another encounter with music. The hunter says, "Please go away," and when the dog asks why he should do so, the answer is, "Don't you

---

[15] Franz Kafka, "Investigations of a Dog," trans. Willa and Edwin Muir, in *Franz Kafka: Collected Stories*, ed. Gabriel Josipovici (New York: Everyman's Library, 1993), 430.

[16] "Small fluffy creatures they perpetually talk about useless philosophical argumentations and observations" (Kafka 1993: 439).

[17] He even asks, "Did they want to lull me to sleep, to divert me, without violence, almost lovingly, from a false path ... ?" And he also goes as far as this following contention: "All knowledge, the totality of all questions and answers, is contained in the dog" (Kafka 1993: 432).

[18] Kafka 1993: 430.

understand the most self-evident fact?"[19] Of course, the self-evident fact is its absence, in the face of which the Hunter starts singing. The problem in the first encounter with the musician dogs is also repeated here: once again, a sonic experience leading to a fundamental question with no answer. As the hunter starts singing, the melody is separated from him and, floating in the air, moves towards the dog.[20] Curiously enough, the hunter "sings without knowing it."[21] In the end, left with no answer to his questions, but at least sensing a proximity between his question about food and music, he decides to conduct some research into the science of music.

Bearing in mind my former discussion on passages and distance, I will propose that the investigations of the dog raise some questions on form, and the audibility of the unformed, leading to an undecidability that I believe prepares some good grounds for us to see the whole story from the viewpoint of what Jean Laplanche called "the enigmatic signifier." In a nutshell, the enigmatic signifier defines a situation where a "whatever signifier" is sent by an adult to be received by an infant as a "whatever signifier," foregrounding a more fundamental question: "What does it mean to receive something?" For Laplanche, "[a]n enigma is not just to ask a question of which you have the answer; it is a question for which even you are not to have an answer."[22] Accordingly, human subjectivity and sexuality are constituted via the infant's attempt at translating such enigmatic messages that are constantly bombarding it. Since these messages are not only linguistic but also include gestures and bodily actions, they always bring about an excess of communication; therefore, Laplanche describes the process as de-translation rather than translation. In other words, even the sender of the message (the adult in this case), as a result of an act of detranslation, can never be sure of what

---

[19] Kafka 1993: 457.
[20] "It grew stronger and stronger; its waxing power seemed to have no limits, and already almost burst my eardrums" (Kafka 1993: 458).
[21] Kafka 1993: 458.
[22] Jean Laplanche, *Seduction, Translation, Drives*, ed. Martin Stanton and John Fletcher, trans. Martin Stanton (London: ICA Press, 1992).

is being sent. Furthermore, the asymmetry of the couple consists of the fact that, in the infant's case, the reception of the enigmatic signifier is what starts the unconscious as a result of primary seduction and repression, whereas the adult has already started this process based on *temporalisation.*

Laplanche, following Freud on seduction theory, claims that sexuality (and therefore the subject) is originally constituted as masochism. It is a self-destructive moment for the subject, and it is masochistic because, right at the instant of its installation—that is, in the face of the enigmatic signifier—the condition of the subject is determined by what he calls "self-shattering." Approaching the matter from a different perspective, Leo Bersani, in his close reading of Freud's *Three Essays on Sexuality,* stresses the destructive but also the productive power of masochism in the constitution of sexuality and the subject as a failure. This point is also there in Laplanche, as a moment of the self-shattering of the ego in the face of an enigmatic message; however, for Bersani, the encounter with the enigmatic signifier in Laplanche leads to a position of paranoid fascination for both parties and therefore remains at a self-destructive level with a claim to knowledge. In his elaboration of Laplanche's seduction theory, Bersani writes:

> Laplanche speaks of this seductive address as an account of the structural formation of the unconscious: primal repression would be the making unconscious of those elements in the enigmatic signifier that infants can't "metabolize," that they are incapable of understanding through some form of symbolization. The implication here is that we are originally seduced into a relation by messages we can't read, enigmatic messages that are perhaps inevitably interpreted as secrets. The result of this original seduction would be a tendency to structure all relations on the basis of an eroticizing mystification. If we feel not only, as Freud proposed, that others threaten the stability the ego must defend for its very survival, but also, more dangerously, that we can be seduced by such threats—in Laplanchian

terms, "shattered into an ego-shattering sexuality"—then it is reasonable to confront others with paranoid mistrust. The enigmatic signifier becomes a knowledge they are at once willfully witholding from me and using in order to invade my being.[23]

Bersani's intention here is to underline the fact that, although Laplanche's theory of seduction is based on a notion of self-shattering, due to its failure to rewrite the masochistic element it involves in terms of the "failure" it proposes, it still carries the promise of knowledge. As he puts it:

Laplanche has formulated a theory of sexual excitement as an effect of *ébranlement*—perturbation or self-shattering—on the organism, an effect that momentarily undoes psychic organization. I have pushed this to the point of arguing, especially in *The Freudian Body*, that sexuality— at least in the mode in which it is constituted—could be thought as a tautology for masochism. In other words, I have been proposing that we think of the sexual—more specifically, of *jouissance* in sexuality—as a defeat of power, a giving up, on the part of an otherwise hyperbolically self-affirming and phallocentricly constituted ego, of its projects of mastery. Thus the subject enters into a Bataille-like "communication with otherness," one in which the individuating boundaries that separate subjects, and that subjects for the most part fiercely defended, are erased.[24]

As can be concluded from above, what is inherently destructive and "promising" in Laplanche is also a mode of survival. For Bersani, "the only way for the infant to survive the imbalance between external stimuli and the ego structures prepared to receive them is to find the pain of this imbalance pleasurable." Further, he writes, "In other words, I am inter-

---

[23] Leo Bersani, "Sociality and Sexuality," *Critical Inquiry* 26 (2003): 641–656.
[24] Bersani 2003: 647–648.

ested in masochism not as pleasure in pain so much as the pleasure of at once losing the self and discovering it elsewhere, inaccurately replicated … . Why is it still masochistic? Because it still means a certain pleasurable renunciation of one's own ego boundaries, the pleasure of a kind of self-obliteration. … I am interested in a pleasure in losing or dissolving the self that is in no way equated with loss, but comes rather through rediscovering the self outside the self."[25]

If we have to summarize the basic distinction between the two, for Laplanche, the unconscious is temporal with a promise of full formation in time, whereas for Bersani the unconscious is spatial: its coming into being cannot be traced, nor can its origin be claimed as the reception of a first signifier—it is conceived as a failure of form.

If the Investigator dog's first encounter with the musician dogs marks an acknowledgement of the Laplanchian enigmatic signifier, his second encounter is stimulated with a desire to destroy this silence and to reach the source of knowledge which, in the end, brings along a shift from food to music, as far as his future researches are concerned. Yet, I believe, a greater shift between two encounters lies in the following: if, in the first encounter, he is alerted to the question of how one receives a message and continues his researches in a paranoid fascination about the origins via preserving a certain distance (positive distance?) from his object in a question-answer dialectics, in the second encounter, just as in Nietzsche's case, he learns to give up his former researches, eliminating even the notion of identification together with that of "distance," and not without a masochistic pleasure in self-shattering or formlessness. Thus, the dog decides to embark upon a new field of research: the science of music. Although he still has some doubts about how to hear it, and fails to identify what he has heard as music, this failure endows him with a freedom from gravity and a movement towards a desire to be a non-localisable, self-floating being in

---

[25] Leo Bersani, "A Conversation with Leo Bersani," *October* 82 (1997): 3–16, 6.

a three-dimensional, rhizomatic space, the truth of which he won't be producing via a paranoid desire to know. As he describes it at the end, it is "a different science from that of today, an ultimate science," as there's nothing to simulate except a sense of a directionless, nomadic floating—not in a mimetic, but rather in a simulacral relationship to "self," much as in a Bataillian mode of communication.

Can this ultimate science be the science of the meta-audible? And if so, what are its conditions?

3. SCHIZO-INCEST

Given this desire for rhizomatic floating with respect to sound or "music," let us look at Deleuze and Guattari's book on Kafka, where they develop the concept of schizo-incest. Initially I shall claim that it is Deleuze's formulation of distance and passage which marks Deleuze and Guattari's determination of two vectorial movements with respect to sound and image in *Kafka: Towards a Minor Literature*,[26] and yet it is also this same approach that short-circuits a more liberatory approach to the relationship between sound and schizo-incest (in other words, when it appears that there are certain stakes in their formulation of movement in a two-dimensional space).

For Deleuze and Guattari, there are two basic fundamental and vectorial moves in Kafka.[27] The bent head/portrait photo is a form of content: "a blocked, oppressed, oppressing, neu-

---

[26] Gilles Deleuze and Félix Guattari, *Kafka: Toward a Minor Literature*, trans. Dana Polan (Minneapolis: University of Minnesota Press, 1986), 68.

[27] "The investigating hound oscillates between two sciences, that of food—a science of the Earth and of the bent head ("Whence does the Earth procure this food?")—and that of music which is a science of the air and of the straightened head, as the seven musical dogs of the beginning and the singing dog of the end well demonstrate. But between the two there is something in common, since food can come from high up and the science of food can only develop through fasting, just as the music is strangely silent" (Deleuze and Guattari 1986: 20).

tralised desire, with a minimum connection, childhood memory, territoriality or reterritorialisation."[28] The straightened head/musical sound, on the other hand, is "a desire that straightens up or moves forward, and opens up to new connections, childhood block or animal block, deterritorialisation."[29] Consequently, when they write about the nature of "music," or sound,[30] in Kafka, their interest focuses on the deterritorializing power of sound: "sound doesn't show up

---

[28] Deleuze and Guattari 1986: 5.

[29] Deleuze and Guattari 1986: 5.

[30] The difference between the two can also be inferred from related pages in *A Thousand Plateaus*, where Deleuze and Guattari develop a distinction between sound and image on the basis of their respective power of deterritorialisation. For them, sound is a more effective element with respect to deterritorialisation:

> But precisely why is the refrain eminently sonorous? Why this privileging of the ear when even animals and birds present us with so many visual, chromatic, postural, and gestural refrains? Does the painter have fewer refrains than the musician? ... There is surely no question here of declaring a given art supreme on the basis of a formal hierarchy of absolute criteria. Our problem is more modest: comparing the powers or coefficients of deterritorialisations of sonorous and visual components. It seems that when sound deterritorialises, it becomes more and more refined; it becomes specialised and autonomous. Colour clings more, not necessarily to the object, but to territoriality. When it deterritorialises, it tends to dissolve, to let itself be steered by other components. This is evident in phenomena of synaesthesia, which are not reducible to a simple colour-sound correspondence; sounds have a piloting role and induce colours that *are superposed* upon the colours we see, lending them a properly sonorous rhythm and movement. Sound owes this power not to signifying or 'communicational' values (which on the contrary presuppose that power), nor to physical properties (which would privilege light over sound), but to a phylogenetic line, a machinic phylum that operates in sound and makes it a cutting edge of deterritorialisation": Gilles Deleuze and Félix Guattari, *A Thousand Plateaus*, trans. Brian Massumi (Minneapolis: University of Minnesota Press, 1987), 347–348.

here as a form of expression, but rather as an *unformed material of expression*, that will act on the other terms."[31] For them, the difference between reterritorialisation and deterritorialisation (as far as sound is concerned) is in fact layered on the distinction or opposition between the formed and the unformed. Hence, when deterritorialisation[32] brings along a total de-structuration of the articulated sound, which in turn is a deterritorialisation and reterritorialisation of noise, this leads to a state of the unformed that is still audible, and of course not as organised music; it is no more a reproduction nor mimesis, nor representational, but a becoming.[33]

Be that as it may, I believe there is a way of challenging this opposition between the formed and the unformed by means of raising the following question: Does Kafka tell us whether this music, song, or whatever can be heard?

One of the finest examples of this issue can be found in "The Silence of the Sirens." Here, Kafka, on the basis of a

---

[31] "What interests Kafka is a pure and intense sonorous material that is always connected *to its own abolition*—a deterritorialized musical sound, a cry that escapes signification, composition, song, words—a sonority that ruptures in order to break away from a chain that is still all too signifying. In sound, intensity alone matters, and such sound is generally monotone and always nonsignifying ... . As long as there is form, there is still reterritorialisation, even in music. In contrast, all of Josephine's art consists in the fact that, not knowing more than the other mice how to sing, she perhaps enacts a deterritorialisation of the 'usual piping' and liberates it from 'the cares of daily life'" (Deleuze and Guattari 1986: 6).

[32] "Since articulated sound was a deterritorialized noise but one that will be reterritoritorialized in sense, it is now sound itself that will be deterritorialized irrevocably, absolutely. The sound or the word that traverses this new deterritorialisation no longer belongs to a language of sense, even though it derives from it, nor is it an organized music or song, even though it might appear to be. ... Everywhere, organized music is traversed by a line of abolition—just as a language of sense is travesed by a line of escape—in order to liberate a living and expressive material that speaks for itself and has no need of being put into form" (Deleuze and Guattari 1986: 21).

[33] See especially Deleuze and Guattari 1987: 13–14.

similar logic that governs the music of the musician dogs in "The Investigations of a Dog," speculates about the silence of the Sirens against their song, the lure of which is determined with a stress on its audibility in the original myth. In Kafka's version of the myth, the Sirens "have a still more fatal weapon than their song, namely their silence."[34] Therefore, when Odysseus passed by them, the Sirens did not sing but "he did not hear their silence; he thought they were singing and ... he alone did not hear them."[35] Or, as Kafka argues, Odysseus might also have noticed that the Sirens did not sing, but he insisted on having heard them as a "shield" against their weapon. Isn't Kafka referring here, against the whole enterprise of interpreting the myth, to the fact that the Sirens' song, because it is based on the formless, cannot be heard? And even when said to have been heard, is this said only as a shield against the inaudibility of the Sirens' song?

I do not propose this point as a matter of conflict in Deleuze and Guattari's theory, but as a way of opening the question of the unformed to the distinction between oedipal- and schizo-incest which, I believe, puts forward a relationship between sound and schizo-incest when some obstacles on the way are cleared. One of these obstacles can be found in Deleuze and Guattari's consideration of the encounter with the Hunter as a moment of reterritorialisation, or a re-Oedipalisation of the dog. As they put it:

> We saw how the animal oscillated between its own becoming-inhuman and an all-too-human familiarization: thus, the dog in "Investigations" is deterritorialized by the musical dogs at the story's beginning, but he is reterritorialized, re-Oedipalized, by the singer-dog of the ending. He ends up oscillating between two "sciences" and is reduced to invoking the eventual coming of a third science that would manage to escape the situation.[36]

---

[34] Kafka 1993: 431.
[35] Kafka 1993: 431.
[36] Deleuze and Guattari 1986: 36.

Although Deleuze and Guattari mention here the liberative power of the ultimate science in future, their claim that the dog is re-Oedipalised with the Hunter scene is without doubt in contrast with what we have said earlier. As we have stated before, the Investigator dog's relation to sound takes place within a three-dimensional free-floating space rather than in a two-dimensional, vectorial one. It is spatial rather than temporal, rhizomatic rather than identical, simulacral rather than mimetic, productively masochistic rather than paranoid, and moves towards the ultimate science: a science of the meta-audible. I want to show here that the liberative power that Deleuze and Guattari assume but defer to a future is already there within their concept of schizo-incest, and what acts as an obstacle is actually their consideration of the Hunter scene not as a deterritorialisation, but as a reterritorialisation. As long as sound is considered in a two-dimensional space, such as liberation, the line of flight will never occur, and it requires a relationship to the unformed, not in a framework of the audible but as a point of undecidability between the audible and the inaudible.

However, in order to show what they claim as reterritorialisation is actually a deterritorialisation opening the dog to a different kind of line of flight, we have to see the distinction they produce between Oedipal- and schizo-incest with respect to image and sound.

In a chapter called "The Connectors" in the Kafka book, Deleuze and Guattari distinguish a class of women who are "part sister, part maid, part whore," who are basically "anti-conjugal, anti-familial,"[37] and who constitute a line of flight from Oedipal familial ties on the basis of "freedom of movement, freedom of statement, freedom of desire."[38] The multiplicity "sister-maid-whore"[39] produces a desire on the basis of

[37] Deleuze and Guattari 1986: 64.
[38] Deleuze and Guattari 1986: 65.
[39] "This combined formula, which has value only as an ensemble, is that of schizo-incest. Psychoanalysis, because it understands nothing, has always confused two sorts of incest: the sister is presented as a substitute for the mother, the maid as a derivative of the mother, the

masochism, so that it not only undoes limitations or rigid subject positions brought along by Oedipal ties, but it also renders possible the other two aspects of freedom. In the first place, in contrast to the neurotic Oedipal incest that occurs with the mother, schizo-incest takes place with the sister and is an incest of deterritorialisation. Belonging to a universal paranoid machine, Oedipal incest has no liberative moment because it falls prey to what has prohibited it—that is, the paranoiac transcendental law—and therefore continuously reterritorializes whatever it has given freedom. Yet what is most striking in their theorisation is the fact that while Oedipal incest is connected to images, schizo-incest is connected to sound with a maximum of connections, and operates on a continuous deterritorialisation towards the unformed, liberating each familial or Oedipal tie from predetermined rules based on a fixed image of thought.[40]

I shall claim at this point that schizo-incest is the con-

---

whore as a reaction-formation. The group of 'sister-maid-whore' will be interpreted as a kind of masochistic detour but, since psychoanalysis also doesn't understand anything about masochism, we don't have to worry much about it either" (Deleuze and Guattari 1986: 66).

[40] "Schizo-incest corresponds to the immanent schizo-law and forms a line of escape instead of a circular reproduction, a progression instead of a transgression ... . Oedipal incest is connected to photos, to portraits, to childhood memories, a false childhoodthat never existed but that catches desire in the trap of representation, cuts it off from allconnections, fixes it onto the mother to render it all the more puerile or spoiled ... . Schizo-incest, in contrast is connected to sound, to the manner in which sound takes flight and in which memory-less childhood blocks introduce themselves in full vitality into the present to activate it, to precipitate it, to multiply its connections. Schizo-incest with a maximum of connection, a polyvocal extension, that uses that uses as an intermediary maids and whores and the place that they occupy in the social series—in opposition to neurotic incest, defined by its suppression of connection, its single signifier, its holding of everything within the limits of the family, its neutralization of any sort of social or political field" (Deleuze and Guattari 1986: 67).

dition of the Investigator dog right after his encounter with the singer-Hunter, especially when his relationship to sound and the unformed is concerned. For one thing, if the dog's approach in his former researches could be named as scientific, tied to a craving for a paranoiac universal truth via scientific methods in a cause-effect relationship, it is undone after the encounter with the Hunter and given another dimension, such as a concentration on music, or the "ultimate science," as the dog puts it. The ultimate science, if it will be a transgressive one, is there in order to deterritorialize what the dog has obtained in his researches until then. Given the dog's desire to be weightless, to reach a nomadic state of floating in the air, we can claim that in this new phase the dog is and will be liberated—or deterritorialized, if you like—on the basis of "freedom of movement, freedom of statement, freedom of desire." His movement will no more be based on a vectorial principle but on a rhizomatic one. His freedom of statement, once the rules of the old science are left behind, will no more be tied to a transcendental paranoiac principle of truth but on a Nietzschean sense of non-topological "distance" from this absent-presence. And finally, his freedom of desire, once he shifts from the science of food to the science of music, will be related to sound, which is not representational but meta-audible, the inaudibility of which, based on a certain masochistic pleasure, will be celebrated as a failure to constitute himself as a full-fledged subject who can "hear" things. Moreover, it is no more a question of the audible by an ear, but by the whole body.

One final point to be made in this context is to show how all this leads Deleuze and Guattari to a different dimension in schizo-incest: namely, "homosexual effusion."[41] After carefully distinguishing "homosexual effusion" from Oedipal homosexuality and also from the multiplicity "sister-maid-whore," they locate it in the homosexual relationship to the artist who has nothing to do with aesthetics, just like other similar figures in Kafka (such as the singer who doesn't know how to

---

[41] Deleuze and Guattari 1986: 68.

sing, or a swimmer who doesn't know how to swim). Yet the artist, "manifestly homosexual,"[42] in whom we can trace a masochistic productivity as far as the dismantling of forms are concerned, is an anti-aesthete and, being so, he "overflows all the segments and sweeps up all the connections"[43] (unlike the "sister-maid-whore alliance," where they observe a move from one segment to another), thereby leading to a "shifting and continuous line of flight."[44]

Together with schizo-incest, doesn't homosexual effusion define a position where even the distinction between the audible and the inaudible disappears, yielding to the meta-audible? And isn't the "ultimate science" of today not even a matter of distance, but of "not to be dead and yet no longer alive," as Nietzsche put it?

---

[42] Deleuze and Guattari 1986: 69.
[43] Deleuze and Guattari 1986: 69.
[44] Deleuze and Guattari 1986: 69.

III: Clinical and Critical Perversion[1]

> The body and mind thereupon become dissociated; the subject crosses the boundary of his own skin and stands outside of his senses. He tries to see himself, from some point in space. He feels that he is turning into space himself—dark space into which things cannot be put.
>
> Roger Caillois, "Mimicry and Legendary Psychasthenia"

0. CRITICAL/CLINICAL

"On the 20th Lenz went through the mountains."[2]

On the 20th of which month?

On the 20th of which month of which year?

Already with the first sentence in his unfinished 1836 novella, *Lenz*, Büchner points not only to the closure of an abyss presumed since Plato to be yawning between two topo-

---

[1] This essay first appeared in *Rhizomes* 26 (2014): http://www.rhizomes.net/issue26/aracagok.html.
[2] Georg Büchner, *Lenz,* in Georg Büchner, *Complete Works and Letters*, trans. Henry J. Schmidt (New York: Continuum, 1991), 139 [139–162].

graphically "indeterminable" edges—between mimesis and diegesis—but also to the difference between the surface and the depths, between the *critical* and the *clinical*. For if it doesn't matter anymore which month of the which year it is, there's only a minimum concern left for the temporal, which, together with the spatial, are the primary constitutive principles of the subject of Enlightenment (a forgetting of remembering, which Adorno and Horkheimer traced even in *The Odyssey*[3]). What this means is that the presumed abyss between mimesis and diegesis, the rejection of which has always been the main concern of the "political" (the repression of which would be the mission of *psychoanalytical* discourse towards the end of the 19th century), is now at stake, as is the constantly upsurging problem of the distinction between the conscious and the unconscious. The distinction between the *immediate* (as in the Kantian problem of the thing-in-itself) and the *mediated* has already found a novel way of expression in *Lenz* as regards the audibility of this "terrible voice which is usually called silence."[4] It is this undecidable question of audibility that I believe raises once again the ungoing question of the political as it is handled by psychiatry in the second half of the 19th century. As will be argued in this chapter, the disappearance of the political, far from being only metaphorical, is basically related to the rise of psychoanalysis (or, rather, psycho-politics) and, being based upon a certain notion of "perversion," it can be re-distributed along Deleuzian distinctions (such as surface and depth, critical and clinical, oedipal-incest and schizo-incest). This could then lead us to a re-evaluation of what Deleuze and Guattari might have meant by "homosexual-effusion" in their book on Kafka,[5] twhich could then

---

[3] Theodor Adorno and Max Horkheimer, "Odysseus or Myth and Enlightenment," *Dialectic of Enlightenment: Philosophical Fragments*, ed. Gunzelin Schmid Noerr, trans. Edmund Jephcott (Stanford: Stanford University Press, 2002), 35–62.

[4] Büchner 1991: 159.

[5] Gilles Deleuze and Félix Guattari, *Kafka: Toward a Minor Literature*, trans. Dana Polan (Minneapolis: University of Minnesota Press, 1986), 36–69.

1. SOMNAMBULISM, HYPNOSIS, AND PSYCHASTHENIA

Ekphrasis 1: Now Lenz is outside in nature, wandering as if under the spell of a fugue, looking for a leak through which he can sneak into space. Knock knock! No phonemes, only their traces ... sonorous but only insofar as the surrounding hum of the world prevents the tympan from shattering. And yet ...

The peaks and high slopes in snow, gray rock down into the valleys, green fields, boulders and pine trees. It was cold and damp, water trickled down the rocks and sprang over the path. Pine branches hung down heavily in the moist air. Gray clouds moved across the sky, but everything so dense, and then the fog steamed up, and trailed, oppressive and damp, through the bushes, so sluggish, so shapeless. He went on indifferently, the path did not matter to him, sometimes up, sometimes down. He felt no fatigue, but at times he was irritated that he could not walk on his head.[6]

On the 20th of which month?
On the 20th of which month of which year?
Already with the first sentence in *Lenz*, Büchner deterritorialises the presumed emotions of the reader into various levels of intensities on the body, without the organs of literature; Lenz is located at a crossroads between psychasthenia and schizophrenia, deterritorialising the politico-topological by playing on the border between the conscious and the unconscious.
If the question is whether the landscape is available as a

---

[6] Büchner 1991: 139.

distinct field of inspection as separate from the traveller, the way Büchner produces an answer to the dichotomy of man and nature offers a strange operation of separation—a separation from a "self" with the intention of melting into landscape—thereby confusing the boundaries between topological and atopological, almost as opposed to, say, Freudian psychoanalysis in the latter part of the 19th century, where the division within the "self" will be attributed to an illness (named "schizophrenia") that unproblematically determines the place where a possible division might have taken place. Or, as the psychotherapists of the the time, Jean-Martin Charcot and Pierre Janet, would have it, it's a case of *dementia*, the symptoms of which are made visible in Lenz's attacks of hysteria and his attempts at self-mutilation, reminiscent of Artaud's, almost a century later. What I will propose here is to unthread Lenz as a possible case of Janet's theory of psychasthenia under a non-psychoanalysing and/or non-Oedipalising light, in order to be able to foreground how the inherent question of the atopological was appropriated by psychoanalysis and transformed into psycho-politics as a result of which perversion is clinicalised. It will also be interesting to note how the profound question of transference was dealt with by Janet and Freud so as not to disturb their theorisation of a self-identical subject—as a failure in the first case, and a success in the latter.

But first of all, let us see briefly what a certain psychological disorder, "psychasthenia," means for Janet, who coined this term for some patients who had symptoms similar to those suffering from "fugue" and "dei paralysis progressiva" (Nietzche's illness, as diagnosed by Doctor Wille[7]) in the 19th century. Psychasthenia, being a form of dementia or dissociation (the earlier names for schizophrenia), represents a disorder in one's spatio-temporal perception, through which one locates oneself in time and space.

---

[7] See Jean Luc Nancy, "Dei Paralysis Progressiva," *The Birth to Presence*, trans. Brian Holmes et al. (Stanford: Stanford University Press, 1993), 48–57.

As his first book *L'Automatisme Psychologique*[8] clearly demonstrates, for Janet there is a profoundly elemental and structural state of mind which is regular and predetermined. In this model there are two basic activities: one preserving and reproducing the past, and the other directed towards synthesis and creation (integration). In other words, the integrative activity organizes the present with its capacity to produce a synthesis that will enable one to readjust one's past experiences within a given changing environment. Such a view on mind led him to a view on hysteria where integrative activity is diminished and can be restored during a hypnotic séance; if such integrative functions are dissociated from the hysteric mind and cause uncontrolled behaviour or perception during crisis, then such dissociation could be cured by way of looking into the causes of trauma in hypnosis. Moreover, for Janet, the patient's suggestibility is in direct proportion to the degree of dissociation, which makes the patient less resistant in hypnosis.

As can be observed from even such a short introduction, Janet's model of mind is basically a Kantian one (which even recalls Hume on the matter of taste), where, given the sound state of well-integrated categories working in harmony, there should be no room for deficiency, especially with regard to a certain, deterministic notion of temporality and spatiality. This is especially evident in Janet's second book *L'Etat Mental des Hysteriques:*[9] "hysteria is a defect of the unity of the mind, manifesting itself on the one hand in a diminishing of the personal synthesis, and on the other, in the preserving of past phenomena which reappear in amplified manner."[10] Although such states of deficiency make patients liable to suggestion,

---

[8] Pierre Janet, *L'Automatisme Psychologique: essai de psychologie expérimentale sur les forms inférieures de l'activité humaine* (Paris: F. Alcan, 1973).
[9] Pierre Janet, *État mental des hystériques: Les stigmates mentau* (Paris: Rueff, 1892).
[10] Onno Van Der Hart and Barbara Friedman, "A Reader's Guide to Pierre Janet on Dissociation: A Neglected Intellectual Heritage," *Dissociation* 2(1): 3–16.

Janet also finds that in cases which are ruled by some fixed ideas, patients can experience a lowered state of suggestibility. In his further researches on the causes and neuroses of fixed ideas, one of the fundamental things he discovers is related to what Freud will later call "transference": an already known state during his time, described as "rapport magiletique" by magnetizers, it involves not only a patient's deep involvement with the therapist but also a keen interest to be hypnotised by the therapist. Soon realising that this can easily turn into an addiction, Janet calls it "la passion somnambulique,"[11] and despite the erotic elements present in this rapport, he prefers to see it in terms of attachment theory: "Such patients not only crave to be hypnotised, but have a permanent need to confess to the psychiatrist whose picture they keep constantly in their subconscious mind, and to be scolded and directed by him."[12] Apparently, Janet, having no concern to psychoanalyse or Oedipalise this problem, turns to a solution that will restore a delicate balance between the patient and the therapist by gradually withdrawing from the guidance process. In a later book, *The Major Symptoms of Hysteria*, he follows the same idea of the human mind being an automaton, complete and well structured at the beginning: "Things happened as if an idea, a partial system of thoughts, emancipated itself, became independent and developed itself on its own account. The result is, on the one hand, that it develops far too much, and on the other hand, that consciousness appears no longer to control it."[13] If, in former research, somnambulism appears as a state of the patient in hypnosis, here it grows into a general symptom of hysteria in which people are so absorbed in their inner experience—caused by an earlier trauma—that a proper contact with external reality is lost. When they rarely

---

[11] Pierre Janet, "L'influence somnambulique et le besoin de direction," *Revue Philosophique* 43(1): 113–143 (also in Pierre Janet, *Névroses et idées fixes*, Vol. 1 [Paris: Félix Alcan, 1898], 423–484).

[12] Henri Ellenberger, *Discovery of the Unconscious: The History and Evolution of Dynamic Psychiatry* (New York: Basic Books, 1970), 369.

[13] Pierre Janet, *The Major Symptoms of Hysteria* (London and New York: Macmillan, 1920), 42.

respond to something in the external world, it is perceived as role-playing within the domain of the inner experience. In other words, when compared to "la passion somnambulique," somnambulism as a symptom of hysteria is ruled by a rejection of mimesis, whereas in the case of treatment by hypnosis, it turns into a passion for obeying a higher voice—that is, playing the role dictated by the therapist. In other words, a somnambulistic tendency, which is regarded as a symptom of an earlier trauma, turns later on into a means of healing under the guidance of a hypnotist-therapist. If dissociation is marked by the absence of such a guidance—that is, with no role to imitate—in hypnosis the situation is reversed by the presence of the hypnotist/theraphist as a model figure. Although this figure proves to be helpful in awakening the somnambulist from his dream world, in the end it leads to some complications in the rapport established between the two. We will look into the nature of this rapport later on and especially into how this will lead Freud from hypnosis to free association ("the talking cure") as a method, but first let us see how Janet defines "psychasthenia," and how its zoological and philosophical implications are worked out by Roger Caillois.

2. BECOMING SPACE

Ekphrasis 2: Nature, described in Lenz is shrinking into a keyhole, and it is as if all the distances disappear, and no in-between is left. Will he be able to be absorbed into space without carrying the flag of mom and dad, state and nation, citizenship and religion, human and all too human?

Everything seemed to him to be so small, so close, so wet, he would have liked to set the earth behind the stove, he could not understand why he needed so much time to climb down a steep slope, to reach a distant point; he felt he should be able to cover any distance in a few steps ...[14]

He thought he must draw the

---

[14] Büchner 1991: 139.

> *storm into himself, contain all within him, he stretched out and lay over the earth, he burrowed into the cosmos, it was a pleasure that hurt him ... but these were only moments, and then he rose, calm, steady, quiet, as if phantoms had passed before him, he remembered nothing.*[15]

According to Janet, if the hysteric's fixed ideas (as in somnambulism) developed completely outside of the individual's personal perception and memory, the obsession of a psychasthenic would take place in collaboration with one's whole personality. Furthermore, it does so without developing itself completely as a fixed idea. Instead, the psychasthenic is continuously doubting his idea. As we stated formerly, Janet's model of mind is based on a certain notion of automatism where all the mental categories work in harmony and produce a perfect synthesis between past and present events. As his work progressed, his experience led him to expand his conceptual model and he developed the ideas of *psychological force* and *tension*[16] as well as a hierarchy of mental functions on five levels, each of which had a coefficient of reality. The highest level of mental activity was the reality function; this is the function of reality in which one grasps the maximum reality of a situation. With respect to this principle of reality, psychasthenia is characterised by a complete loss of reality, or the loss of reality as an idea, where, such a loss becoming the arche-fixation, the psychasthenic refuses to engage with reality in an integrative way, and resistd producing a synthesis between past and future.

If psychasthenia in Janet is an ultimate form of dissoc-

---

[15] Büchner 1991: 140.

[16] See Pierre Janet, *La Force et la faiblesse psychologique* (Paris: Maloine, 1932).

iation, the main symptom of which is somnambulism where the patient is in a state of hypnosis with no one to mime, no model to imitate, or, better, where any form of role playing or imitation which establishes "reality" *as such* is out of question, I'd like to claim at this point, together with Caillois, that what is at stake here is a certain relationship to the "spatial." As I will have more opportunity to stress later on, our understanding of time and space is still conditioned within Kantian approaches, according to which time and space are *a priori* mental categories. Seen in a line of continuity with the Descartian and Kantian subject, Janet's model of mind is based on an autonomous subject who is supposed to locate him/herself according to these *a priori* mental categories if this subject wants to stay away from the fallacy of reason, if it has to construct a reality *as such*, if it has to stay away from the *clinical*. In contrast, I will argue an understanding of time and place not as *a priori* mental categories but as those whose construction is experienced as always-at-stake and requires a critical mind (rather than "clinical") which has a special relationship with the spatial (one of the underlying definitions of "perversion" by Freud). Moreover, I will claim that, with regard to *Lenz*, Freud's theorisation of perversion is aware of the fact that perversion is what dislocates a certain sense of spatio-temporal relationality, which balances the social, the psychological, and the political, and, therefore, the measures taken against this threat start with the question of the "homosexual."

First, in order to open this mimetic subjectivity to a critique, we might turn to Roger Caillois's essay, "Mimicry and Legendary Psychasthenia," where he suggests an anti-mimetic, or, rather, an ultra-mimetic moment that rejects the distinction between mimesis and diegesis. Discussing the Darwinian postulation of the survival of the fittest with respect to "adaptation," Caillois argues that, due to an absolute, ultra-mimetic representation of the environment, of the space where the same species become their own predators, mimetic adaptation in the insect world does not always lead to survival and can instead lead to death.[17] Basing his argument on the fact that the insect world works on smell rather than sight, Caillois claims that mimicry does not function as a means of the survival of the fittest, working instead as a means of absorption into space on the basis of an *"attractio similium* of magic: *like produces like."*[18] Caillois refers to sympathetic magic, thereby evoking shamanism where the possessed shaman passes from imitating the spirit he's representing to becoming the spirit itself. If, in other words, nature is the shaman, the insects go back to it as if to catch "the sorcerer in his own trap,"[19] realising a complete *"depersonalisation through assimilation into space."*[20] In this atopological topography where any concern for spatio-temporal concern disappears, "Matters become critical with represented space because the living creature, the organism, is no longer located at the origin of the co-ordinate system but is simply one point among many. Dispossessed of its privilege, it quite literally *no longer knows what to do with itself.*"[21]

3. Perversion Clinicalised

Ekphrasis 3: Oberlin the Father is also possessed with nature, and possession takes the form of a voice heard at night; he tells Lenz *how he had heard a voice, how it had spoken to him at night, and how God*

It had grown dark, heaven and earth melted together. It seemed as if something were following him, as if something horrible would overtake him, something that humans cannot endure, as if insanity were

---

[17] "We are therefore dealing with a *luxury* and even with a dangerous luxury, as it does occur that mimicry makes the mimetic creature's condition worse": Roger Caillois, "Mimicry and Legendary Psychasthenia," *The Edge of Surrealism*, ed. Claudine Frank, trans. Claudine Frank and Camille Naish (Durham: Duke University Press, 2003), 91–103, emphasis in original.
[18] Caillois 2003: 97–99.
[19] Caillois 2003: 97.
[20] Caillois 2003: 100, emphasis in original.
[21] Caillois 2003: 99, emphasis in original.

had entered him so completely that he took his Bible verse upon which Lenz is struck— how close nature came to this people.[22]

pursuing him on horseback.[23]

The urge in him, the music, the pain shattered him. For him there were wounds in the universe; he felt deep, inexpressible grief because of it. Now, another existence, diving, twitching lips bent over him and sucked his lips; he went up to his lonely room. He was alone, alone![24]

Do animals have moral codes with respect to perversion?

Is perversion a rejection of being foregrounded as a species—with "species" here understood as a moral concept?

I ask these question immediately at the beginning of a section named "perversion" not only because they are, for the time being, dimly related to our ongoing discussion in this chapter, but also because they reflect the underlying core postulations, or the *mentalité*, of the people working on psychiatry in the 19th century. Despite the Cartesian dictum according to which man is distinguished from the animal on the basis of an ability to speak, 19th-century psychiatric research was riddled with comparisons between man and the animal, especially where the question of sexuality was concerned. For example, on the basis of its presumed presence in both man and animal, what is called the "sexual instinct" was considered during that time as natural or normal if and only if it yielded in the end to "propogation,"[25] and anything that

---

[22] Büchner 1991: 143.
[23] Büchner 1991: 140.
[24] Büchner 1991: 144.
[25] See, for example, Richard Von Krafft-Ebing, *Psychopathia Sexualis, with Especial Reference to the Antipathic Sexual Instinct: A Medico-Forensic Study*, trans. Franklin S. Klaf (New York: Bell Publishing Co, 1965), 34–36.

deviated from this pathos would be named "perversion." In other words, the "naturalness" of the animal world, where there is supposed to be no perversion, and sexual instinct has only the natural function of propagation, was taken as a model of normality for the man; meanwhile, it is forgotten that perversion as a clinical term is applicable only to those who have a sense of a norm, a normality. If 19th-century psychiatry formulated perversion with regard to reproduction, it did so not only within a framework of moral codes (highly determined by rigid concepts of religion, humanity, and normality), but also in an easily maintained series of comparisons between man and animal with respect to the Descartian "rational man." So, given such a stronghold of "naturalness" and "normality" in 19th-century psychiatry, it does not come as a surprise to see Freud referring to this widely appreciated view already in the first two paragraphs of the first essay in *Three Essays on the Theory of Sexuality*:

> The fact of the existence of sexual needs in human beings and animals is expressed in biology by the assumption of a "sexual instinct," on the analogy of the instinct of nutrition, that is of hunger.[26]

However, in just the next paragraph he merely states the following caution:

> We have every reason to believe, however, that these views give a very false picture of the true situation. If we look into them more closely we shall find that they contain a number of events, inaccuracies and hasty conclusions.[27]

Given this conclusion, one immediately wonders whether

---

[26] Sigmund Freud, "Three Essays on the Theory of Sexuality," Vol. 7, *The Standard Edition of the Complete Psychological Works of Sigmund Freud*, trans. and ed. James Strachey and Anna Freud (London: Hogarth, 1953-1974), 135–162.

[27] Freud 1953: 135.

Freud is not quite convinced with the popular opinion of the time, and therefore will challenge this aforementioned "normality" where the animal is appropriated into a model after the application of human moral codes. What happens instead is the introduction of two technical terms, "the sexual object" and "sexual aim," which determine the route of the sexual instinct directly from one to another; if the sexual object is "the person from whom sexual attraction proceeds," the sexual aim is "the act towards which the instinct tends."[28] Yet, as the next sections of the first essay bear witness, Freud doesn't stop there. After a discussion about the choice of children and animals as sexual objects, he introduces a shocking novelty into the widely held beliefs of the 19th century, and changes his position as follows:

> It has been brought to our notice that we have been in the habit of regarding the connection between the sexual instinct and the sexual object as more intimate than it in fact is. Experience of the cases that are considered abnormal has shown us that in them the sexual instinct and the sexual object are merely soldered together—a fact which we have been in danger of overlooking in consequence of the uniformity of the normal picture, where the object appears to form part and parcel of the instinct. We are thus warned to loosen the bond that exists in our thought between instinct and object. It seems probable that the sexual instinct is in the first instance independent of its object; nor is its origin likely to be due to its object's attractions.[29]

What has happened in between? Has Freud realised now the dangers of appropriation of the animal as a model, and therefore he is trying to devise some way of getting rid of this model? Or, given the exact correspondence between sexual object and sexual aim based on propagation, does he think he

---

[28] Freud 1953: 135–136.
[29] Freud 1953: 147–148.

won't have enough space for speculation for his upcoming psychoanalytical theory where the norm will be established on the *self-identical individual* who becomes what he is via eliminating each and every possible tie to nature/animal, especially on the basis of diegesis, and thus embraces an identity free of the animal—a purely restricted Oedipal economy of man as against the non-mimetic, unlocalisable general economy?

Of course, things do not happen in one night, and before seeing how this concern about the self-identical subject of psychoanalysis will lead Freud to a shift from hypnosis to association as a method of treatment, let us see what happens later on in *Three Essays*. Now, if the sexual instinct is declared to be independent of its object, Freud had to invent a normalising process—that is, the *Oedipal family*—that will shift the focus from natural/animal to the boundaries of the family. As is well known, one of the main contributions of *Three Essays* is that that "perversion" was present even among the healthy, and that the path towards a mature and normal sexual attitude began not at puberty but at early childhood. Looking at children, Freud claimed to find a number of practices that looked innocuous, but were really forms of sexual activity, among which thumb sucking was a primary example. Such a consideration, therefore, would lead Freud to the conclusion that "the sexual instinct itself may be no simple thing, but put together from components which have come apart again in the perversions."[30] These components, then, will be said to function anarchically until the primacy of the genital zone is established. If, for example, practices like thumb sucking and kissing are thought to be perversions in previous sections, it is mainly because such diverse components of the sexual instinct present since early childhood will be normalised in time, and will leave their places to the constitution of more proper erotogenic zones, which are the male and female genital organs. As Freud put it:

> If a perversion, instead of appearing merely *alongside* the

[30] Freud 1953: 162.

normal sexual aim and object, and only when circumstances are unfavourable to *them,* and favourable to *it*—if, instead of this, it ousts them completely and takes their place in all circumstances—if, in short, a perversion has the characteristics of exclusiveness and fixation—then we shall usually be justified in regarding it as a pathological symptom.[31]

This is all to say that perversions present since early childhood are negligible until they become the determining factor of a presupposed normality, which is supposed to constitute its erotogenic zones via an Oedipal education of genital organs. This move spectacularly explains why Freud detaches sexual instinct from its object first, if only be able to give it to the service of a guiding principle of topologically determinable erotogenic zones. Hence, perversion, though untied from a certain sexual object, will now become *clinical* per se.

As will be seen in the next section, Freud will draw the boundaries between mimetic and diegetic with his theory of transference, where the Oedipal determinations, achieved by a shift from hypnosis to association, will foreground *representation* as the essential form of the subject and the unconscious. It is with this shift that Freud will be able to clinicalise perversion as a question of localisability, visibility, and audibility. In contrast, the distribution of the genital zone over the whole body, transforming the whole body into a force field of intensities, would undoubtedly undo the question of localisability.

Freudian determinations are therefore Kantian ones, where temporal and spatial determinations constitute the subject in conformity with a certain notion of the *Gestalt*. But what if, as Roger Caillois has shown, there are not only some animal species but also some particular cases in human species that consider *Gestalt* as redundant? In other words, what if psychasthenia is not only a symptom of an illness, but presents a liberative, critical moment which can be considered

---

[31] Freud 1953: 161, emphasis in original.

as psychosis only within a general economy of bourgeois psychoanalysis?

Will transference be eliminated so that the constitutive critical perversion will be clinicalised?

Will Lenz be absorbed into psychasthenia, or, being clinicalised, will he efface the critical position he raises in the history of literature?

4. SCHIZO-INCEST, HOMOSEXUAL-EFFUSION, AND CRITICAL PERVERSION

Ekphrasis 4: Lenz rejects his father's calls. He does not want to go back home, to the house of Oedipus. Instead, hovering above the clusters of realism, he invents schizo-incest and Oberlin simply responds with kisses.

... he believed it must be boundless ecstasy to be touched in this way by the unique life of every form; to commune with rocks, metals, water, and plants; to assimilate each being in nature as in a dream, as flowers take in air with the waxing and waning of the moon.[32]

When he was alone, or reading, it was even worse, at times all his mental activity would hang on one thought; if he thought about or visualised another person vividly, it seemed as if he were becoming that person, he became utterly confused, and at the same time he had a boundless urge to internalise everything around him arbitrarily.[33]

---

[32] Büchner 1991: 145.
[33] Büchner 1991: 157.

> *... you see, Pastor, if only I didn't have to hear that anymore, that would do me good. "Hear what my friend?" Don't you hear anything, don't you hear the terrible voice, usually called silence, screaming around the entire horizon, ever since I've been in this silent valley I always hear it ...* [34]

According to Mikkel-Borch Jacobsen,[35] although Freud rejects hypnosis with a preference for free association, he never succeeds in eliminating the question of transference. What is decisive about this rejection is the distinction between mimesis and diegesis, which can be separated along the lines of enactment/catharsis and narrative. However, what comes to the fore as his analysis of hysteria develops is the impossibility of undermining "the emotional tie,"[36] and thus the question of

---

[34] "Hören Sie denn nichts? Hören Sie denn nicht die entsetzliche Stimme, die um den ganzen Horizont schreit und die man gewöhnlich die Stille heißt? Seit ich in dem stillen Tal bin, hör ich's immer, es läßt mich nicht schlafen; ja, Herr Pfarrer, wenn ich wieder einmal schlafen" (Büchner 1991: 159).

[35] Mikkel Borch-Jacobsen, *The Emotional Tie: Psychoanalysis, Mimesis and Affect*, trans. Douglas Brick et al. (Stanford: Stanford University Press, 1993).

[36] As Borch-Jacobsen puts it, the "emotional tie" as the bond that develops between the analysand and the analyst during treatment is what complicates the identity of psychoanalysis; this is related to what Freud calls "primary identification" or "incorporation" (Borch-Jacobsen 1993: 39):

> Yet this 'emotional tie,' which certainly remains very close to the 'hypnotic tie,' still cannot be represented or remembered, if only it precedes the ego, the-subject-of-the-representation .... "Identification," Freud says in *Group Psychology*, "is the original form of emotional tie with an object," and this means that the ego forms itself or is *born* in this devouring identification with the

"transference" as the emotional tie is the pivot which preconditions one's relation to the Other and is pre-psychoanalytical and pre-representational at the same time. In other words, transference is elusive because it both constructs and deconstructs the subject of psychoanalysis. As will be seen below, transference, making the subject hear the voice of the silence—that is, as in Lenz's case—brings along an invitation to a psychasthenic universe where one no longer knows where one is.

At this juncture, I'd like to go back to the question of the audible in Lenz we mentioned at the beginning of this chapter and suggest that it is actually against this becoming-audible of silence—that Lenz has heard—that 19th-century psychiatry and psychoanalysis slowly developed a tendency to put a ban on the voice of the analyst. If in Charcot and Janet the question of transference is negligible to a certain extent, it is because they, unlike Freud, do not have an overall theory of the subject or psyche based on Oedipal norms. For Freud, the voice of the analyst in a hypnotic séance opens the doors towards making the patient hear the voice of the silence;[37] in a hypnotic séance, the voice of the analyst, replicating the voice of the Other, reaches the innermost boundaries of the subject, and then violates and shakes them down to their foundations.

> other ... This first "emotional tie" to another, which is also the unrepreentable event of my "own" birth, can never be remembered, never be recalled to memory. This is also why it can never be "dissolved," as Freud would have it. But (and this is what happens all the time, if it happens) it can be *repeated*—for example, in hypnotic trance, or in the oblivion of transference. In the end, in this strange rite of passage that today we call 'psychoanalysis,' perhaps the only stake is this: repeating, repeating the other in oneself, dying to oneself—to be reborn, perhaps, *other*.
> (Borch-Jacobsen 1993: 60–61)

[37] As Mladen Dolar discusses, for Freud, the drives are silent, and it is only the libido which can speak in the face of an attempt on the part of the analysand who restructures a language of his/her own during the therapy where the analyst adopts a stance of silence: Mladen Dolar, *A Voice and Nothing More* (Cambridge: M.I.T. Press, 2006).

In contrast, during the "talking-cure," the Freudian subject should reintegrate his/her fallen boundaries if s/he has to reconstruct his/her integrity along the lines of the Oedipal family.

Discussing the availability of transference in the matter of distinguishing analysis from hypnosis, Jacobsen draws up a framework for Freudian psychoanalysis where the traces of the emotional tie can be found in any kind of relationship, which is basically hypnotic *per se*. Furthermore, hypnosis calls for a cathartic enactment which debases any notion of the self-identical subject by opening it to an invasion by the other. In other words, the analysand enacts the traumatic scene by re-living it in a mimetic (not diegetic) fashion—he or she becomes someone else at the moment of enactment—and this state is induced by the voice/suggestions of the analyst. This double invasion disturbs all the spatio-temporal relationship of the self to itself: first as letting oneself be invaded by the voice/suggestion of the analyst, and then as becoming someone else in enactment under hypnosis. The supposed cure is the enactment of the very scene initiated by this double invasion, where the analysand's relationship to time and space is interrupted with a concern for treatment.

The emotional tie, for Jacobsen, is thus a "rapport without rapport"[38] where a concern for the topological is undermined by the de/constitutive role it plays in the attainment of the subject *as such*. The emotional tie, in this sense, triggers an understanding of perversion as a sexual instinct which does not have any *a priori* object of love. But before that, we should ask if there are possible ways of approximating the emotional tie with perversion on the basis of mimesis. If mimesis is opposed to diegesis (for not being a narration or representation but becoming one with the one that one identifies with), then there arises a situation where the "I" or ego *as such* does not exist. Not having an "I" means not only not being introduced to time and space, but also a moment of "becoming-mimesis" itself where the object of love is put at stake,

---

[38] Borch-Jacobsen 1993: 42.

never being able to appear *as such*. It is a desire not only with no fixed object, but also with no object where the boundaries between object and subject have disappeared.

When hypnosis is understood as Mikkel Borch-Jacobsen understands it (as a destructive strategy for Freudian psychoanalysis based on the self-preservation of the subject), "perversion" present in a hypnotic séance or in *la passion somnambulique* (as for Janet) becomes constitutive; although it yields to an unceasing transference between the analyst and the analysand during the séance, it can be tolerated until the "sound" state is maintained. It is right here at this moment (what Deleuze and Guattari call "schizo-incest" in their book on Kafka[39]) that the sound state becomes central in our ongoing discussion on constitutive/critical perversion. What if such a sound state is never maintained, and the analysand is given the freedom of enjoying his/her perversion critically before s/he is captured by the *machine-clinique*?

Schizo-incest, according to Deleuze and Guattari, is the distribution of a relationality, not on the basis of Oedipal ties but as an alliance of brothers and sisters against the mom and dad. Eventually, it is not based on a mimetic model-copy relationship but rather, if we may say so, on a simulacral relationship where identity is always at stake or fails to produce identifications. It is a state that precludes Freudian psychoanalysis, where the emotional tie is not yet captured by, and is not yet invested in, an Oedipal machine ... no identification occurs there (in the absence of an ego)—or, better, there is an identification, but since the model cannot be remembered and represented, it never reaches the point of an *aufhebung* where it will produce "mother" and "father" as exact figures of identification. We have seen formerly how the "enigmatic signifier" of Laplanche[40] is taken by Bersani[41] to

---

[39] Deleuze and Guattari 1986: 68.
[40] Jean Laplanche, *Seduction, Translation, Drives*, ed. Martin Stanton and John Fletcher, trans. Martin Stanton (London: ICA Press, 1992).
[41] See Leo Bersani, "Sociality and Sexuality," *Critical Inquiry* 26 (2003): 641–656.

force a celebration of failure. What I propose here is to insert Bersani's non-relational relationality (obtained as a result of the affirmation of failure—the "masochistic pleasure," if you like) into *la passion somnambulique*, where the emotional tie, given the freedom to fail, establishes a rapport without a rapport in the absence of fixed identites. This ultimately gives the lie to any theory of self-identity that works on the gestalt of Kantian spatio-temporality. Without doubt, here we are talking about a Deleuzian desiring-machine with no fixed object on which it invests its love, but also about the affirmation of psychasthenia as a critical position that can only be obtained by an affirmation of perversion as the de/constitutive principle of the "ego."

If heterosexual love is possible only where identites are fixed or distributed along the lines of Oedipalised genders, what Deleuze and Guattari describe as "homosexual effusion" most likely delineates a horizontal expansion saturated with sound (noise? clamour?), only—as against the specular—a surface effect with no depth, as Deleuze explains so well in *The Logic of Sense*.[42] Moreover, as it is construed in their Kafka book, "homosexual effusion" is an expression-machine that connects singularities on the basis of a perversion-machine: a critique of identity that centres around expression rather than aesthetics. Yes, the voice/sound/noise still exist here, but having denied any transcending transcendental, they can never be tied to a composition, a song, or a melody orchestrated by the voices of god, or mom, or dad. Critical perversion appropriates only the clusters of a vague rhythm that date back to a primary "emotional tie," whose clamorous echoes of refrain can never be heard in the dark corridors of identity. It has no relation with the specular nor with the speculative insofar as the maintenance of the "political" is concerned. All because, 0) the critical perversion is rooted in psychasthenia, and, n–1) to hear the voice of the silence is the failure to remember the

---

[42] Gilles Deleuze, *The Logic of Sense*, ed. Constantin Boundas, trans. Mark Lester and Charles Stivale (London: Continuum, 2003), 158–178.

primary emotional tie, the remembrance of which territorialises and reterritorialises "politics" over and over again today. What we need today is to deterritorialize politics.

Clinical perversion topologically connects one only to the one and single machine—the Oedipal-machine—whereas critical perversion, having multiple connection points, is atopological. It starts with schizo-incest and homosexual effusion, yet the ultimate point is the bachelor-machine. In fact, nothing describes critical perversion better than the "bachelor-machines" that Deleuze and Guattari talk about at the end of their chapter, "The Connectors," in *Kafka: Toward a Minor Literature*:

> In fact, these connector characters, with their connotations of desire, incest, or homosexuality, receive their objective nature from the machine of expression, and not the other way around … . No one knew better than Kafka to define art or expression without any sort of reference to the aesthetic. If we try to sum up the nature of the artistic machine of Kafka, we must say that it is a bachelor machine, and, as such, plugged all the more into a social field with multiple connections. Machinic definition and not an aesthetic one. The bachelor is a state of desire much larger and more intense than incestous desire and homosexual desire … . His trips aren't those of the bourgeoisie on an ocean-liner … but the schizo-voyage … . His voyage is a line of escape … . He doesn't flee the world; he grasps it and makes it take flight on a continuous and artistic line … . With no family, no conjugality, the bachelor is all the more social, social-dangerous, social-traitor, a collective in himself … . The highest desire desires both to be alone and to be connected to all the machines of desire. A machine that is all the more social and collective insofar as it is solitary, a bachelor, and that, tracing the line of escape, is equivalent in itself to a community whose conditions haven't yet been established.[43]

---

[43] Deleuze and Guattari 1986: 70–71.

Now, have we fallen outside psychoanalysis?

I have only tried to foreground a new constellation—that is, clinical perversion with a clinically perverted desire for schizo-incest, homosexual effusion, and bachelor-machines.

References

Adorno, Theodor and Max Horkheimer. "Odysseus or Myth and Enlightenment." In *Dialectic of Enlightenment: Philosophical Fragments*, ed. Gunzelin Schmid Noerr, trans. Edmund Jephcott, 35–62. Stanford: Stanford University Press, 2002.

Bersani, Leo. "A Conversation with Leo Bersani." *October* 82 (1997): 3–16.

Bersani, Leo. "Sociality and Sexuality." *Critical Inquiry* 26 (2003): 641–656.

Borch-Jacobsen, Mikkel. *The Emotional Tie: Psychoanalysis, Mimesis and Affect*, trans. Douglas Brick et al. Stanford: Stanford University Press, 1993.

Büchner, Georg. *Lenz*, in Georg Büchner, *Complete Works and Letters*, trans. Henry J. Schmidt, 139–162. New York: Continuum, 1991.

Caillois, Roger. "Mimicry and Legendary Psychasthenia." In Roger Caillois, *The Edge of Surrealism*, ed. Claudine Frank, trans. Claudine Frank and Camille Naish, 91–103. Durham: Duke University Press, 2003.

Deleuze, Gilles. "Letter to a Harsh Critic." In Gilles Deleuze,

Negotiations, trans. Martin Joughin, 6. New York: Columbia University Press, 1995.

Deleuze, Gilles. *The Logic of Sense*, ed. Constantin Boundas, trans. Mark Lester and Charles Stivale. London: Continuum, 2003.

Deleuze, Gilles and Félix Guattari. *Kafka: Toward a Minor Literature*, trans. Dana Polan. Minneapolis: University of Minnesota Press, 1986.

Deleuze, Gilles and Félix Guattari. *A Thousand Plateaus*, trans. Brian Massumi. Minneapolis: University of Minnesota Press, 1987.

Dolar, Mladen. *A Voice and Nothing More*. Cambridge: M.I.T. Press, 2006.

Ellenberger, Henri. *Discovery of the Unconscious: The History and Evolution of Dynamic Psychiatry*. New York: Basic Books, 1970.

Freud, Sigmund. "Three Essays on the Theory of Sexuality." In *The Standard Edition of the Complete Psychological Works of Sigmund Freud*, Vol. 7, ed. and trans. James Strachey and Anna Freud, 135–162. London: Hogarth, 1953.

Kafka, Franz. "Investigations of a Dog," trans. Willa and Edwin Muir. In *Franz Kafka: Collected Stories*, ed. Gabriel Josipovici, 430–458. New York: Everyman's Library, 1993.

Janet, Pierre. *État mental des hystériques: Les stigmates mentau*. Paris: Rueff, 1892.

Janet, Pierre. *Névroses et idées fixes*, Vol. 1 (Paris: Félix Alcan, 1898).

Janet, Pierre. *The Major Symptoms of Hysteria*. London: Macmillan, 1920.

Janet, Pierre. *La Force et la faiblesse psychologique*. Paris: Maloine, 1932.

Janet, Pierre. *L'Automatisme Psychologique: essai de psychologie expérimentale sur les forms inférieures de l'activité humaine*. Paris: Félix Alcan, 1973.

Janet, Pierre. "L'influence somnambulique et le besoin de direction." *Revue Philosophique* 43.1 (1897): 113–143.

Laplanche, Jean. *Seduction, Translation, Drives*, ed. Martin Stanton and John Fletcher, trans. Martin Stanton. London:

ICA Press, 1992.

Nancy, Jean-Luc. "Dei Paralysis Progressiva." In Jean-Luc Nancy, *The Birth to Presence*, trans. Brian Holmes et al., 48–57. Stanford: Stanford University Press, 1993.

Nietzsche, Friedrich. *The Gay Science*, trans. Walter Kaufmann. New York: Vintage Books, 1974.

Plotnitsky, Arkady. *The Knowable and the Unknowable*. Ann Arbor: University of Michigan Press, 2002.

Van Der Hart, Onno and Barbara Friedman. "A Reader's Guide to Pierre Janet on Dissociation: A Neglected Intellectual Heritage." *Dissociation* 2.1 (1989): 3–16.

Von Krafft-Ebing, Richard. *Psychopathia Sexualis, with Especial Reference to the Antipathic Sexual Instinct: A Medico-Forensic Study*, trans. Franklin S. Klaf. New York: Bell Publishing Co., 1965.

ABOUT THE AUTHOR

Zafer Aracagök is an academic and musician who teaches art theory and continental philosophy at Bilgi University, Istanbul, Turkey. He is the author of three books (in Turkish) and a number of articles addressing the issues of image, resonance, and noise in continental philosophy and especially in the philosophy of Deleuze and Guattari in academic journals such as *Revue Chimères, Pli: The Warwick Journal of Philosophy, Parallax, Third Text, rhizomes, Postmodern Culture* and *Symploke*. His book, *Desonance: Desonating (with) Deleuze*, was published in 2009. His musical work has been released and performed both in Turkey and abroad, such as in the UK, France, Germany and Italy. Aracagök organised "Resonances: A Deleuze and Guattari Conference on Philosophy, Arts and Politics" at Bilgi University in July 2010, and he edited a special issue on Deleuze and Guattari for *Parallax* (Routledge, 2012). His most recent work is *I Want to be a Suicide Bomber* (Little Black Cart, 2013). He is also one of the advisory editors of *rhizomes: cultural studies in emerging knowledge* (http://www.rhizomes.net).

W. dreams, like Phaedrus, of an army of thinker-friends, thinker-lovers. He dreams of a thought-army, a thought-pack, which would storm the philosophical Houses of Parliament. He dreams of Tartars from the philosophical steppes, of thought-barbarians, thought-outsiders. What distance would shine in their eyes!

~Lars Iyer

www.babelworkinggroup.org

www.ingramcontent.com/pod-product-compliance
Lightning Source LLC
Chambersburg PA
CBHW070849160426
43192CB00012B/2369